Microsoft®
Access 2002
fast&easy®

Check the Web for Updates:

To check for updates or corrections relevant to this book and/or CD-ROM visit our updates page on the Web at **http://www.prima-tech.com/support/**.

Send Us Your Comments:

To comment on this book or any other PRIMA TECH title, visit our reader response page on the Web at **http://www.prima-tech.com/comments**.

How to Order:

For information on quantity discounts, contact the publisher: Prima Publishing, P.O. Box 1260BK, Rocklin, CA 95677-1260; (916) 787-7000. On your letterhead, include information concerning the intended use of the books and the number of books you want to purchase. For individual orders, turn to the back of this book for more information.

Microsoft® Access 2002

fast&easy®

Faithe Wempen

A DIVISION OF PRIMA PUBLISHING

A Division of Prima Publishing

Prima Publishing and colophon and Fast & Easy are registered trademarks of Prima Communications, Inc. PRIMA TECH is a trademark of Prima Communications, Inc., Roseville, California 95661.

Publisher: Stacy L. Hiquet
Managing Editor: Sandy Doell
Acquisitions Editor: Deborah F. Abshier
Project Editor: Melba Hopper
Technical Reviewer: Patrice-Anne Rutledge
Copy Editor: Melba Hopper
Interior Layout: LJ Graphics, Susan Honeywell
Cover Design: Prima Design Team
Indexer: Johnna VanHoose Dinse

ISBN: 0-7615-33958
Library of Congress Catalog Card Number: 20-01086687
Printed in the United States of America

00 01 02 03 04 DD 10 9 8 7 6 5 4 3 2 1

To Margaret

Acknowledgments

Thanks to the great editorial staff at Prima Publishing, whose names appear on the Credits page, for all their hard work.

About the Author

Faithe Wempen, M.A., is an A+ certified PC technician and a Microsoft Office Authorized Instructor. She owns and operates Your Computer Friend, a training and troubleshooting business in Indianapolis, Indiana, and is the author of more than 50 books on computer hardware and software.

Contents at a Glance

Contents

Introduction

Access is one of the world's most popular database systems, and Access 2002 is part of the Microsoft Office XP suite. Using Access, you can create sophisticated and powerful databases and store and analyze information on any number of topics. For many beginning computer users, however, database programs seem complicated and intimidating. But they needn't be.

Access 2002 Fast & Easy isn't designed to provide comprehensive coverage on every aspect of Access. Instead, it focuses on the best way to do essential tasks and provides step-by-step visual instructions on how to do these tasks. Using this approach makes creating a database both fast and easy.

What's New in Access 2002?

Access 2002 offers improvements over previous versions of the program both in power and in usability. For the professional database developer, Access 2002 offers unparalleled Web integration capability, along with features that enable SQL and Access to work together. (*SQL* is a database format in use at many large corporations; it is expected to eventually replace Access as the tool of choice for large databases.) For the beginner or casual user, Access 2002 includes more automated procedures, more Wizards that walk you step-by-step through complex activities, and easier-to-understand instructions and messages. In addition, like all the other Office 2002 programs, Access uses a task pane to provide quick access to common program features.

Who Should Read This Book?

Access 2002 Fast & Easy is a visual guide, created for people who learn best by seeing a representation of what they're doing. This book is directed at beginning to intermediate computer users, particularly those new to Access. More experienced users who prefer a visual, hands-on approach might also benefit from this book. If you want to look and learn without having to wade through a lot of text and technical detail, then this book is for you.

Added Advice to Make You a Pro

Access 2002 Fast & Easy provides a step-by-step, sequential approach to learning. Starting at the very beginning, the book guides you through the creation of an entire relational database system. Along the way, you'll discover several elements that help you increase your knowledge and proficiency.

- Tips provide hints on ways to make common tasks even easier or suggest shortcuts for these tasks.

- Notes offer useful background information, advice, or suggestions that will help you learn more about the program.

- Cautions keep you on your toes by notifying you of potential pitfalls and hazards that might hinder your process.

In addition, the book contains four appendixes, each with specialized information you might want:

- Appendix A covers installing Access 2002 and Office XP and adding or removing program features.

- Appendix B provides a basic tutorial of menus, toolbars, and the Help system for those who are just starting out with computers.

- Appendix C lists keyboard shortcuts you might find useful.

- Appendix D explains the principles of good database design.

- The Glossary provides definitions of important Access terminology.

I hope you enjoy reading and using *Access 2002 Fast & Easy!*

PART I

Getting Started with Access

1

Starting and Exiting Access

Access 2002, which is part of the Microsoft Office XP suite, is one of the most popular and powerful database applications available. Using Access, you can easily create a relational database that includes data entry forms, reports, and queries. In this chapter, you'll learn how to:

- Start Access
- Exit Access

Starting Access

Depending on the options you choose when you install Access, the menu path you use to start Access might differ slightly.

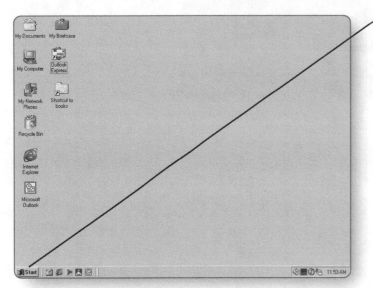

1. **Click** on the **Start button**, located in the lower-left corner of the screen. The Start menu will appear.

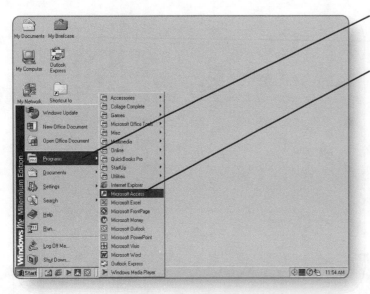

2. **Click** on **Programs**. The Programs menu will appear.

3. **Click** on **Microsoft Access**.

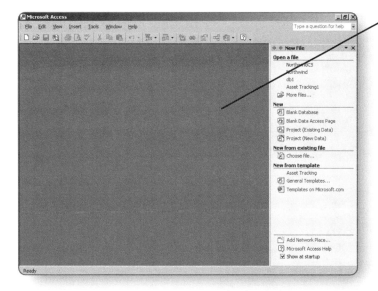

The Microsoft Access window will open.

NOTE

If this is your first time using a Microsoft Office program, check out Appendix B, "Office Program Basics," for help with menus, toolbars, and other features common to all Microsoft Office programs.

Exiting Access

When you finish working in Access, be sure to exit the program properly to avoid damaging your database.

1. Click on **File**. The File menu will appear.

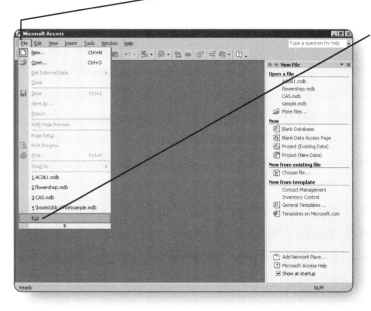

2a. Click on **Exit**. Access will close, and you will return to the Windows desktop.

OR

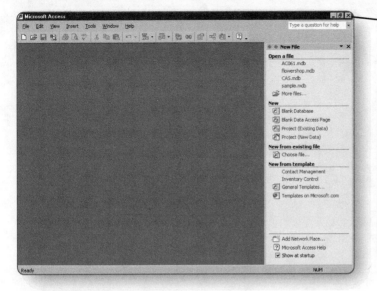

2b. Click on the **Close button** as an alternate way to exit Access in only one step.

NOTE

Access saves your changes automatically when you exit the program or close a database, so you do not have to issue a command to save your work before exiting.

2

Creating a New Database

You can create a new database either from scratch (a blank database) or based on a template provided with Access. If you use a template, the Database Wizard guides you through the creation of a basic set of tables, forms, and reports appropriate to the chosen template, such as contact management or order entry. If you start with a blank database, you create each object in the database separately, as later chapters will explain. In this chapter, you'll learn how to:

- Create a database using a template
- Work with a Switchboard
- Create a blank database

Creating a Database from a Template

When you base a new database on a template, the Database Wizard walks you step-by-step through a process of choosing a template, creating a database file, and choosing the database fields and other customization. It also builds several tables, forms, queries, and reports for your use automatically.

Displaying the Task Pane

The task pane, which appears automatically when you start Access, offers shortcuts for creating new databases. If the task pane is not visible, display it.

1. **Click** on the **New button** on the toolbar. The task pane will appear (if it is not already visible).

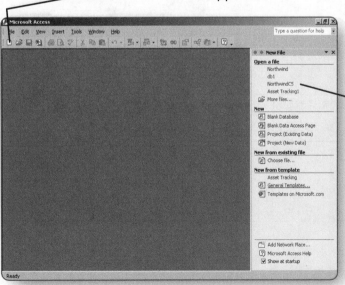

NOTE

If you (or anyone) have used Access on your PC before, the task pane will show shortcuts to previously created databases and previously used templates. The shortcuts on your task pane might be different than some of the ones shown here.

Starting a Database from a Template

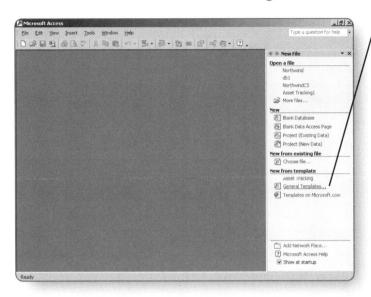

1. Click on **General Templates** in the task pane. The Templates dialog box will open.

2. Click on the **Databases tab** if it is not already selected. The contents of the Databases tab will display.

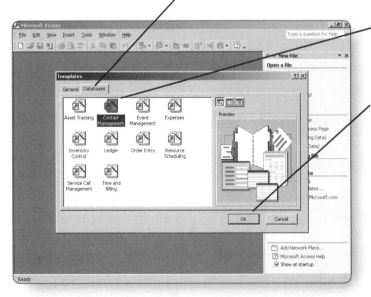

3. Click on the **template** you want to use. The template will be highlighted.

4. Click on **OK**. The File New Database dialog box will open.

5. Choose a **different file location** if you want to save the file in a folder other than the default folder (C:\My Documents).

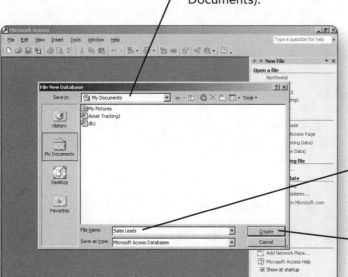

NOTE

If you are not familiar with navigating files and folders, refer to Appendix B, "Office Program Basics."

6. Enter a **name** for the new database in the File name text box.

7. Click on **Create**. The Database Wizard will open.

TIP

In Access, you enter a name for your database when you first create it, and Access saves your work automatically under that name as you work.

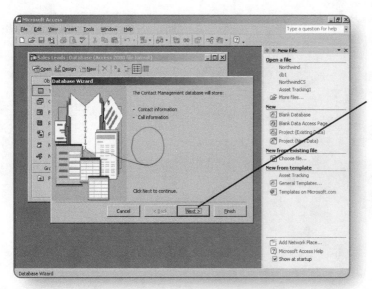

8. Click on **Next** to continue.

Selecting Database Fields

The Database Wizard does not allow you to modify the core list of fields that comes with each sample table, but it does enable you to choose whether you want certain optional fields to be included.

A database can contain one or more tables, each with numerous fields.

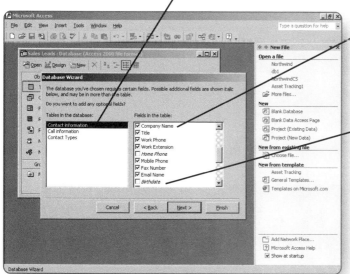

The fields you'll probably want to have in your tables are already selected. You cannot deselect them.

Optional fields that you might want to consider are not automatically selected and are listed in italics. You can click to place a check mark next to any of these.

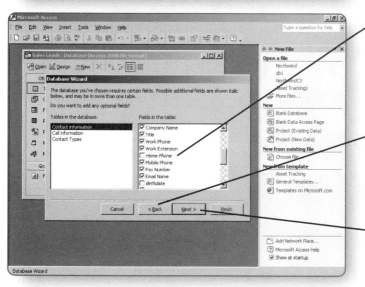

1. Click on the **check box** next to any additional field that you want to include in your table.

TIP

You can click on the Back button to return to the previous wizard step at any point in the process.

2. Click on **Next** to continue.

Customizing the Database

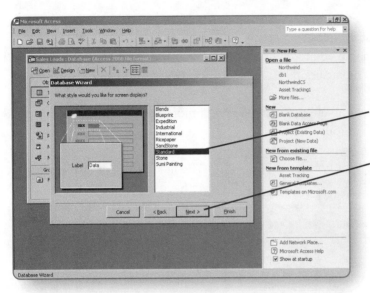

Next, you'll customize your database by choosing styles for screens and reports. You'll also add a title to your database.

1. **Click** on the **style** that you want to use in database screens.

2. **Click** on **Next** to continue.

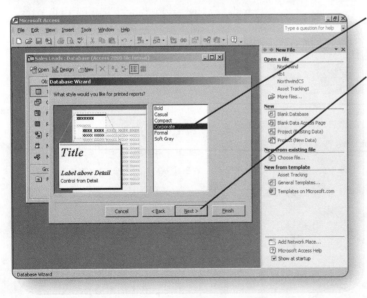

3. **Click** on the **style** that you want to use in printed reports.

4. **Click** on **Next**.

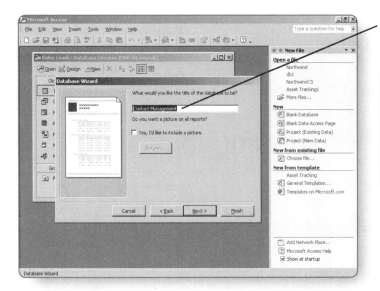

5. **Enter** the **title of your database** in the text box.

NOTE

This is the title that appears on database objects—not the file name for the database.

Adding a Picture or Logo to Reports

You can also add pictures, such as a company logo, to your reports. If you have a small graphic stored on your hard disk containing your company's logo, you can tell the Database Wizard to insert it on the reports that it creates.

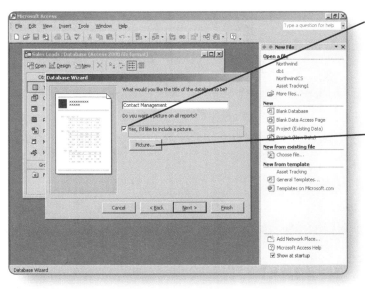

1. **Click** on the **Yes, I'd like to include a picture check box** to include a picture on your reports. The Picture button will activate.

2. **Click** on the **Picture button**. The Insert Picture dialog box will open.

3. Choose a **different file location** if needed to locate the file.

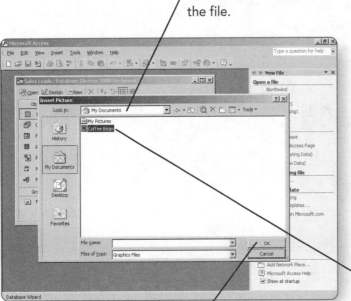

NOTE

Depending on where the picture is stored on your hard disk or network, you might need to navigate to a different folder. You can choose a different drive from the Look in drop-down list. See "Browsing for File Locations" in Appendix B for help.

4. Click on the **name of the picture** you want to insert.

5. Click on **OK**.

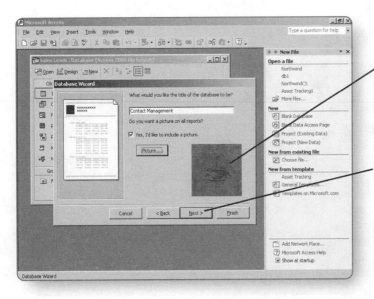

NOTE

A sample of the image will appear in the Database Wizard.

6. Click on **Next** to continue.

Finishing the Database

After selecting a name and a picture (if desired), click on Finish to tell Access to build the database using your specifications.

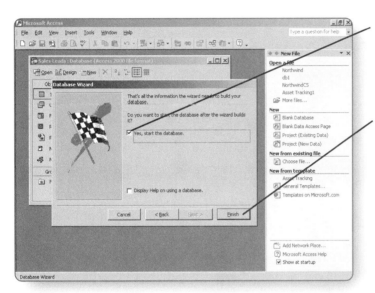

1. Click on the **Yes, start the database check box** to start the database when you finish the Database Wizard.

2. Click on **Finish**. The Database Wizard will build the database.

Working with a Switchboard

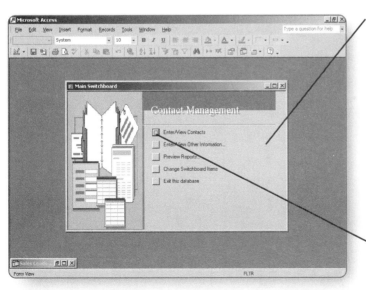

A database you build with the Database Wizard displays a form called the Main Switchboard. This form includes buttons that help you navigate around your database without having to use the main database window. Using the Main Switchboard, you can enter and view data using forms, print reports, and more.

1. Click on a **button on the Switchboard**. A form, report, or other object will appear for your use.

Closing the Switchboard

The Switchboard is most useful for someone who wants to use the database to enter records, run reports, and other routine activities. Much of this book focuses on setting up a database, so you will probably want to turn off the Switchboard for greater control over the database tables, forms, and other objects.

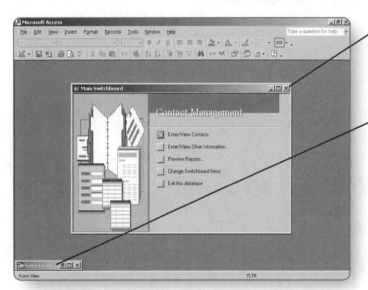

1. Click on the **Close button** on the Switchboard window. The Switchboard window will close.

2. Double-click on the **minimized database window**. The database window will appear.

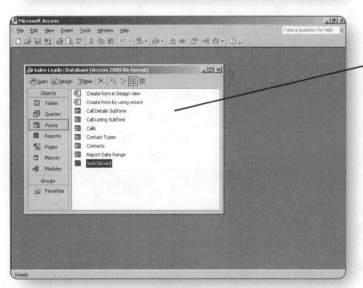

NOTE

The database window is the central point for creating, modifying, and deleting all types of objects in a database, including tables, forms, reports, and so on. You will work with it throughout the remainder of this book.

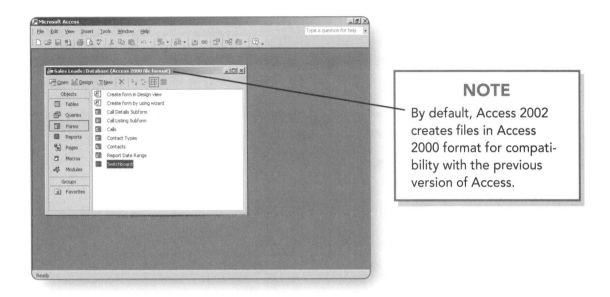

NOTE

By default, Access 2002 creates files in Access 2000 format for compatibility with the previous version of Access.

Creating a Blank Database

If you don't want to use the Database Wizard, you can create a database from scratch. You can then manually add your own tables, forms, queries, and reports to it, as explained in Parts II through VI of the book.

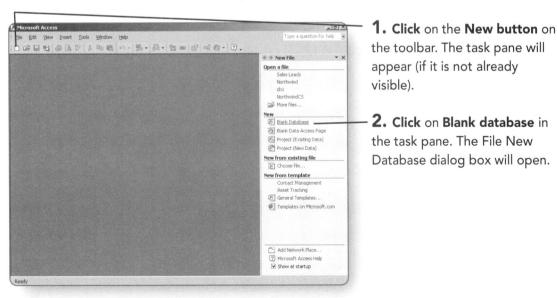

1. **Click** on the **New button** on the toolbar. The task pane will appear (if it is not already visible).

2. **Click** on **Blank database** in the task pane. The File New Database dialog box will open.

NOTE

If you do not want to save the file in the default location (C:\My Documents), you can choose a different drive or folder.

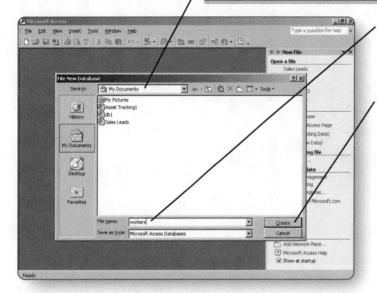

3. Enter a **file name** for the database in the File name text box.

4. Click on **Create**. A blank database will appear.

3

Opening and Using Databases

Once you create a database in Access, you'll want to open it again and again. You'll also need to familiarize yourself with the Database Window before you start working with tables, reports, queries, and forms within the database. In this chapter, you'll learn how to:

- Open an existing database
- Understand the Database Window
- Use the Database Window

Opening a Recently Used Database

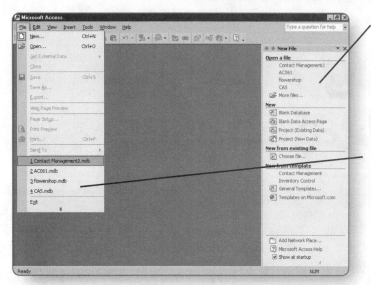

The task pane provides quick access to any of the last four databases you have used. To reopen one of those databases, simply click the database name on the task pane.

The same four databases appear at the bottom of the File menu; you can also select them from there.

Opening an Existing Database

If the database you want does not appear on the list of recently used databases, you must use the Open dialog box to find and open the database.

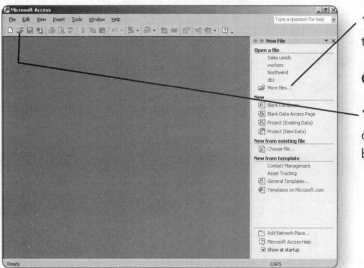

1a. **Click** on **More files** in the task pane.

OR

1b. **Click** on the **Open button** on the toolbar. The Open dialog box will appear.

TIP

You can also open the File menu and choose the Open command for Step 1.

2. Click on the **folder** that contains the database you want to open. See Appendix B, "Office Program Basics," for help if needed.

3. Click on the **database file name** you want to open.

4. Click on the **Open button**. The database will appear in the Access window.

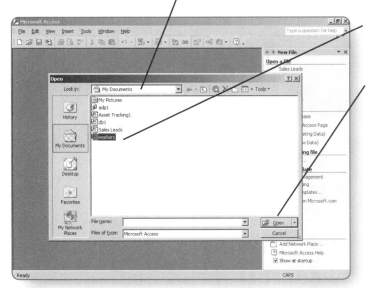

NOTE

If you open a database that contains a Switchboard, the Switchboard will open, and the main database window will be minimized. See Chapter 2, "Creating a New Database," for help closing the Switchboard and displaying the database window.

Understanding the Database Window

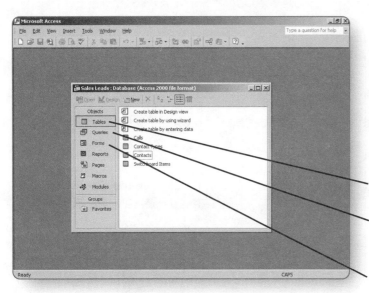

The left side of the database window includes seven buttons, each corresponding to one of the seven objects that make up an Access database. A database is essentially a collection of information. In an Access database, you do the following:

Collect information in tables.

Query tables to analyze their content.

Enter information into these tables by using forms.

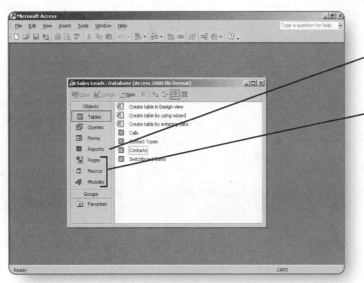

Create reports based on the tables and queries.

As an advanced user, you might also design data access pages to view your Access data from the Web, create macros to automate tasks, or create modules to build database applications using Access.

Using the Database Window

After you open a database, you can open or create tables, queries, forms, reports, and pages.

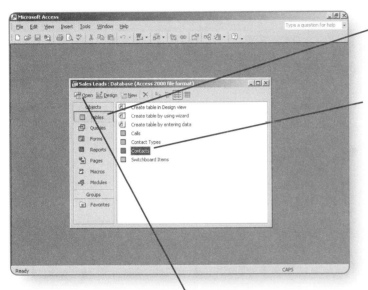

1. Click on the **object button** you want to view. A list of the available objects will appear.

2. Click on the **object** you want to access.

3a. Click on **Open** to open a table or query in Datasheet view, a form in Form view, or a page in Page view.

OR

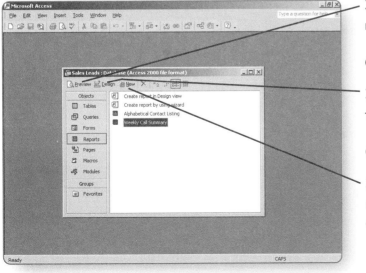

3b. Click on **Preview** to view a report.

OR

3c. Click on **Design** to display the object in Design view.

OR

3d. Click on **New** to create a new database object. The New dialog box will open.

TIP

You can double-click on any object to open or preview it, combining Steps 2 and 3a or 3b into a single action.

Deleting an Object in the Database Window

You can delete an object that you created by mistake or that you no longer need from within the Database Window.

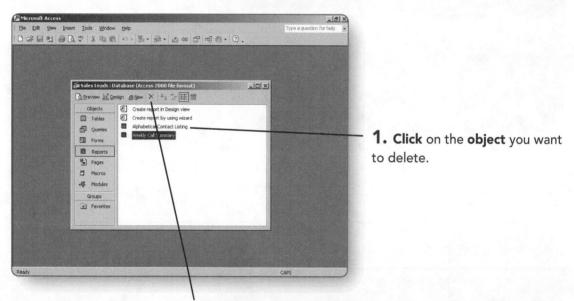

1. Click on the **object** you want to delete.

2. Click on the **Delete button** on the database toolbar. A confirmation box will appear.

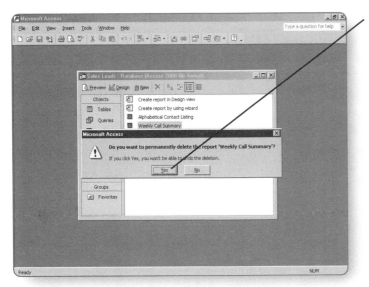

3. Click on **Yes** to confirm. The object will be deleted.

CAUTION

Deleted items are not retrievable; you can't undo a deletion. In addition, any other objects that rely on the deleted object will cease to work (such as a form based on a deleted table).

Viewing Objects in the Database Window

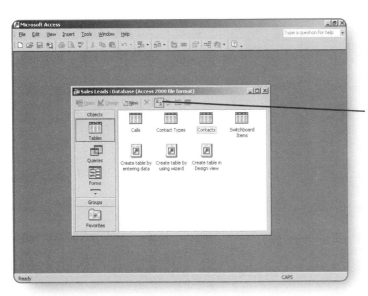

The Database Window includes four buttons that determine how you view available objects in this window.

Click on the Large Icons button to view all objects as large icons.

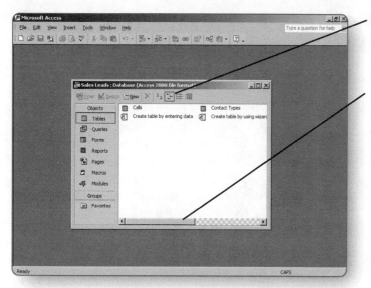

Click on the Small Icons button to view all objects as small icons in horizontal rows.

Use the bottom scroll bar to scroll to the left or right to see the rest of the list.

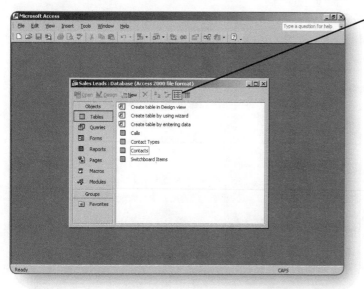

Click on the List button to view all objects as small icons in vertical columns. This is the default viewing option.

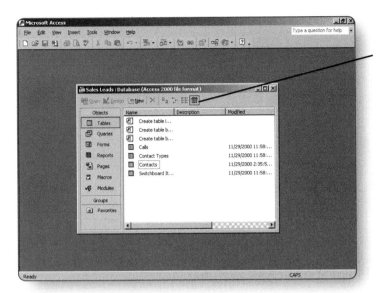

Click on the Details button to view a list of details next to each object. This list provides a description of the object, the date you last modified it, the date you created it, and the type of object it is.

Part I Review Questions

1. What are two ways to exit from Access? *See "Exiting Access" in Chapter 1*

2. What benefit do you get from creating a new database from a template rather than creating a blank one? *See "Creating a Database from a Template" in Chapter 2*

3. How do you display the task pane if it is not already visible? *See "Displaying the Task Pane" in Chapter 2*

4. When using the Database Wizard to select fields for your tables, what does an italicized field name indicate? *See "Selecting Database Fields" in Chapter 2*

5. What is a Switchboard? *See "Working with a Switchboard" in Chapter 2*

6. What is the easiest way to reopen a database that you worked with the last time you used Access? *See "Opening a Recently Used Database" in Chapter 3*

7. If the database you wanted did not appear on the task pane, how would you display the Open dialog box to locate it? *See "Opening an Existing Database" in Chapter 3*

8. Name the seven types of objects you can create in the database window. *See "Understanding the Database Window" in Chapter 3*

9. When you double-click on a table in the database window, what happens? *See "Using the Database Window" in Chapter 3*

10. What's the difference between Small Icons view and List view? *See "Viewing Objects in the Database Window" in Chapter 3*

P A R T   I I

Working with Tables

4

Creating a Table with the Table Wizard

The Access Table Wizard offers an easy way to create your own tables, in addition to those that the Database Wizard might have created initially. Access includes numerous table templates that you can use to create both business and personal database tables. Access also provides step-by-step guidance as you create your database. In this chapter, you'll learn how to:

- Start the Table Wizard
- Choose table fields
- Name the table and set a key
- Set table relationships
- Finish the table

Starting the Table Wizard

The Table Wizard can help you create common types of tables, including those that store mailing lists, recipes, investments, video collections, invoices, or exercise logs.

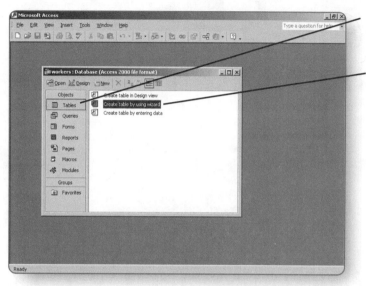

1. **Click** on the **Tables button** in the main database window.

2. **Double-click** on the **Create table by using wizard option**. The Table Wizard will appear.

Choosing Table Fields

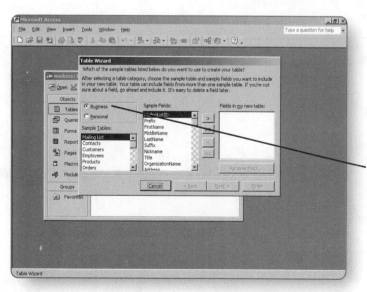

Next, you choose the specific fields for your table. You can easily modify the sample tables by selecting only certain fields or by renaming the fields to something that's more appropriate for your needs.

1a. **Click** on the **Business option button**. Sample business tables will appear in the Sample Tables scroll box.

OR

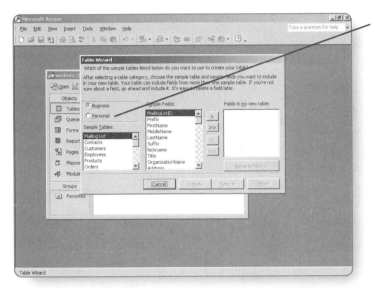

1b. **Click** on the **Personal option button**. Sample personal tables will appear in the Sample Tables scroll box.

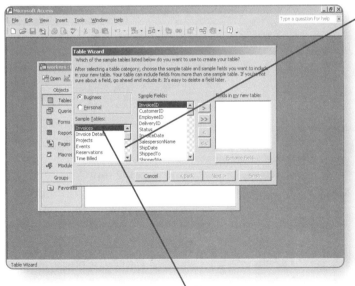

2. **Scroll down** the Sample Tables scroll box until you see the sample table you want to use.

3. **Click** on this **sample table**. Sample fields, based on the table you choose, will appear in the Sample Fields scroll box.

4. Click on a **field** from the Sample Fields scroll box that you want to include in your table. The field will be selected.

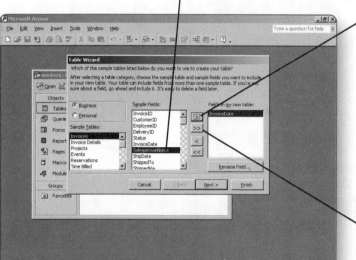

5. Click on the **right arrow button**. The sample field will move to the Fields in the new table scroll box.

6. Repeat Steps 3, 4, and **5** until you've selected all the sample fields you want to include in your table.

TIP

Click on the double right arrow to include all sample fields in your table.

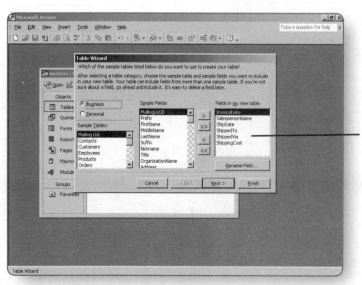

Removing Fields

You can easily remove fields that you have selected to include in your new table.

1. Scroll down the **Fields in my new table scroll box** until you see the field you want to remove.

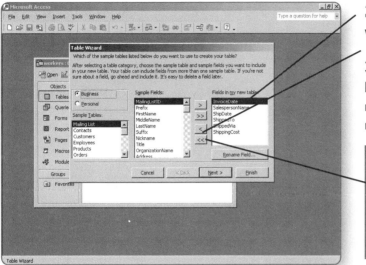

2. Click on this **field**. The field will be selected.

3. Click on the **left arrow button**. The field will be removed from the Fields in my new table scroll box.

TIP

Click on the double left arrow to remove all the fields in the Fields in my new table scroll box.

Renaming Fields

You can rename a field after you move it to the Fields in my new table scroll box.

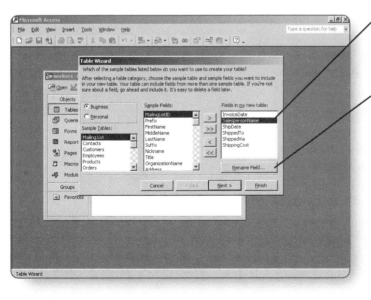

1. Click on the **field** you want to rename in the Fields in my new table scroll box.

2. Click on **Rename Field**. The Rename field dialog box will open.

3. Enter the **new name** for the field in the Rename field text box.

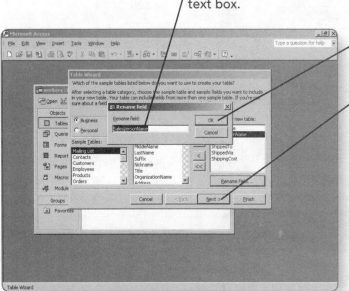

4. Click on **OK**. You will return to the Table Wizard.

5. Click on **Next**. The Table Wizard will continue to the next step.

Naming the Table and Setting a Key

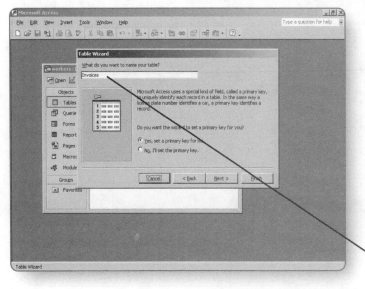

In this step of the Table Wizard, you name your table and determine how to set a primary key. A *primary key* is an important concept in relational database design. This key provides a unique tag for each row in your table, called a *record*. Access uses this primary key to relate the records in this table to another table in your database.

1. Enter a **name** for your table in the text box.

TIP

A table name can have up to 64 characters, including letters, numbers, and spaces. Creating meaningful names for all parts of your database—tables, reports, forms, and queries—will help make it easier to use and manage.

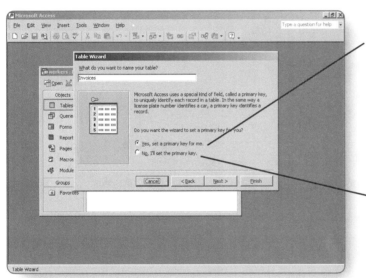

2. Click on the **Yes, set a primary key for me option button**. A primary key will automatically be set.

NOTE

The easiest way to set a primary key is to let Access set it for you. If you want to set your own key, click on the No, I'll set the primary key option button. The Table Wizard opens a new dialog box in which you can choose how to set the primary key yourself.

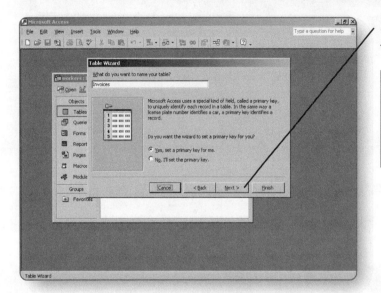

3. Click on **Next** to continue to the next step.

> ### TIP
> Click on the Back button to return to the previous wizard step.

Setting Table Relationships

In a relational database, you will want to relate the data from one table to another. For example, you might have a master Customers table and another table for individual Orders. You'll enter each customer once in the Customers table, but enter the customer many times in the Orders table as he or she places multiple orders. Each of these tables will have a field to identify the customer, and it is this field that relates the tables to each other.

> ### NOTE
> You will see this step only if your database already contains at least one table. If this is the first table you are creating, you will skip this step.

Click on Next if your new table isn't related to any existing tables. If you want to relate your new table to an existing one, Access can create the relationship for you.

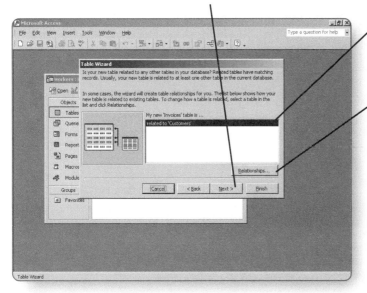

1. Click on the **name of the existing table** you want to relate to your new table.

2. Click on **Relationships**. The Relationships dialog box will open.

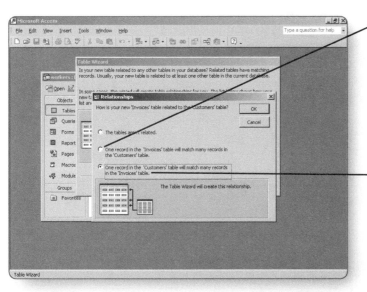

3a. **Click** on the **One record in the 'Invoices' table will match many records in the 'Customers' table option button**.

OR

3b. **Click** on the **One record in the 'Customers' table will match many records in the 'Invoices' table option button**.

NOTE

The one-to-many distinction is very important in setting table relationships. Remember that the "one record" table should be the one with unique values for that field. For example, you would list each customer once in a Customers table and many times in an Invoices table.

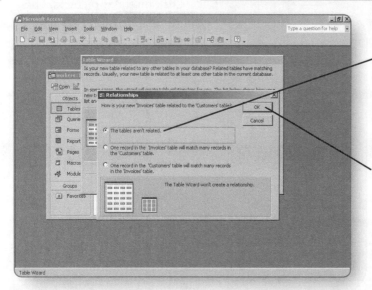

TIP

Click on The tables aren't related option button to undo a table relationship you previously made.

4. Click on **OK**. You will return to the Table Wizard.

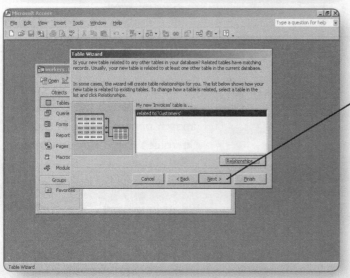

5. Click on **Next**. You will continue to the next step.

Finishing the Table

In the last step of the Table Wizard, you determine how you want to view your completed table.

1a. Click on the **Modify the table design option button**. The table will open in Design view.

OR

1b. Click on **the Enter data directly into the table option button**. The table will open in Datasheet view.

OR

1c. Click on the **Enter data into the table using a form the wizard creates for me option button**. A form for entering data into your table will open.

2. Click on **Finish**.

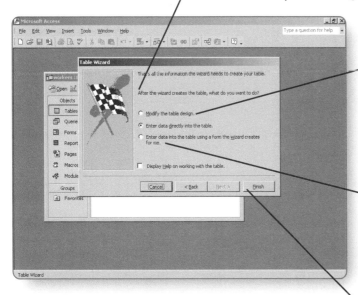

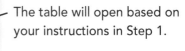

The table will open based on your instructions in Step 1.

5

Creating a Table from Scratch

If you want more control over table creation than the Table Wizard provides or if you just want to try creating a table from scratch, Access offers two different ways to do so. In this chapter, you will learn how to:

- Create a table in Datasheet view
- Create a table in Design view

Creating a Table in Datasheet View

Datasheet view provides a quick way to create a new table using a spreadsheet-like grid of rows and columns. It's a simple, non-intimidating way for beginners to build a table. Access automatically assigns the data types (text, numbers, dates, and so on) based on the data you enter. When you save a table created in Datasheet view, Access also asks whether you want to create a *primary key*, a field that is unique to each record of the table.

Access assigns default field names such as Field1, Field2, and so on, but you will probably want to rename the fields to more useful names. When choosing field names for your table, keep in mind that Access field names are restricted to 64 or fewer characters. You can include:

- Letters of the alphabet

- Numbers

- Special characters, except for a period, an exclamation point, an accent grave, or brackets

- Spaces, provided you are not going to use the field name in an expression or in Visual Basic, both of which are advanced features of Access

1. Click on the **Tables button** in the main database window.

2. Click on **New**. The New Table dialog box will open.

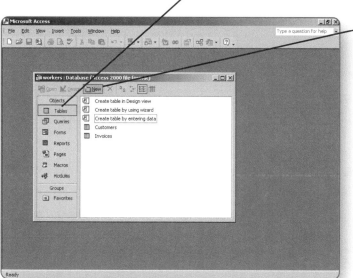

3. Click on the **Datasheet View option**.

4. Click on **OK**. A blank table will open in Datasheet view.

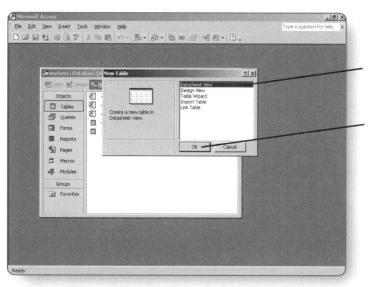

5. Enter the **desired data** into your table.

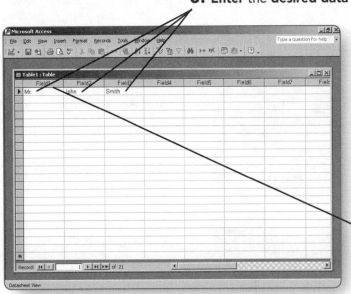

6. Click on the **column header** of the first column you want to rename. The column will be selected and will turn black.

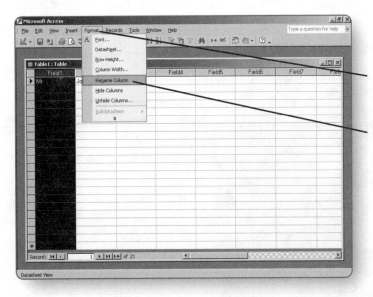

7. Click on **Format**. The Format menu will appear.

8. Click on **Rename Column**. The column header name will be selected.

TIP
You can also double-click on the column header instead of doing Steps 7 and 8.

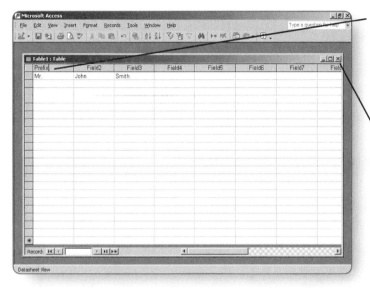

9. Type a **new column name**.

10. Repeat Steps 6 through **9** until you have renamed all the columns that you want to use.

11. Click on the **Close button**. A dialog box will open asking if you want to save your new table.

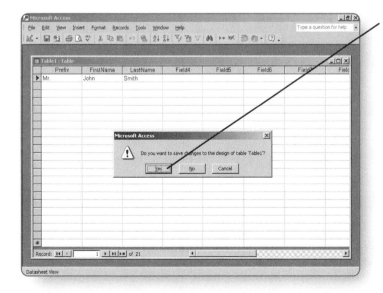

12. Click on **Yes**. The Save As dialog box will open.

13. **Enter** the **name of your table** in the Table Name text box.

14. **Click** on **OK**. A dialog box will open asking if you want to create a primary key.

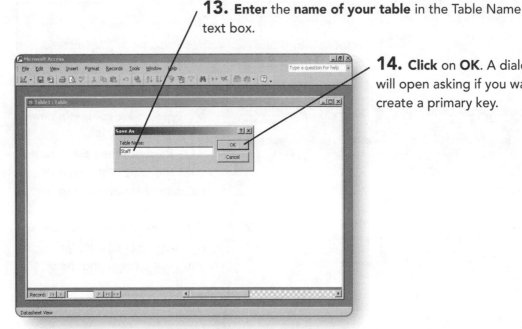

15. **Click** on **Yes**. The main database window will appear. You can now open your new table in Design view to look at the automatic defaults and make any additional modifications, such as changing a data type or adding a description.

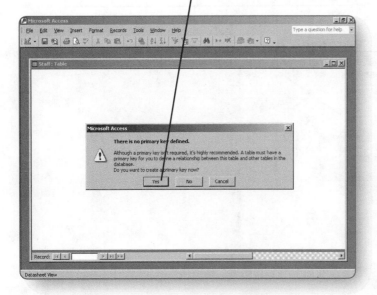

TIP

By default, a table you create in Datasheet view includes 10 fields. If you don't need all 10, you can delete unnecessary fields by selecting them and choosing Edit, Delete Column. When you save and close the datasheet, Access automatically deletes columns that you didn't name.

Creating a Table in Design View

To gain even greater control over how you create your table, you can create it in Design view. In Design view, you enter your own field names and descriptions and choose your own data type to associate with each field. You can also set your own primary key.

Before creating a table entirely from scratch, you should write your basic table structure on paper, focusing particularly on field names and data types.

Access fields can have one of the following data types:

- **Text**. Stores text or combinations of text and numbers— such as addresses—up to 255 characters.

- **Memo**. Stores text and numbers up to 65,536 characters; used for detailed, descriptive fields.

- **Number**. Stores numeric data that you can use in calculations.

- **Date/Time**. Stores a field in date or time format.

- **Currency**. Stores currency data that you can use in calculations.

- **AutoNumber**. Stores a sequential number for each record.

- **Yes/No**. Stores only one of two values such as Yes/No, True/False, or On/Off.

- **OLE Object**. Stores objects created in another application—such as Word or Excel—that you can link to or embed in an Access table.

- **Hyperlink**. Stores a link to a Web page, e-mail address, or another object in the database.

- **Lookup Wizard**. Stores a lookup column that you can reference from another table.

1. Click on the **Tables button** in the main database window.

2. Click on **New**. The New Table dialog box will open.

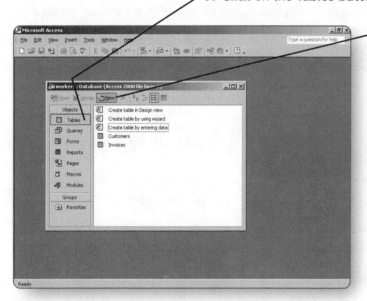

3. Click on **Design View**.

4. Click on **OK**. A blank table will open in Design view.

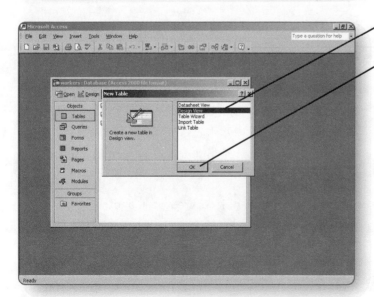

5. **Enter** the **first field name** in the Field Name column.

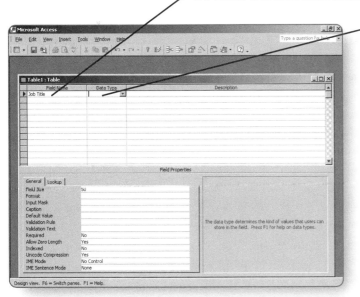

6. **Press** the **Tab key** to move to the Data Type column.

NOTE
"Text" appears in the Data Type column by default, but you can choose any of the 10 different data types for your field.

7. **Click** on the **down arrow** to the right of the field. A list of available data types will appear.

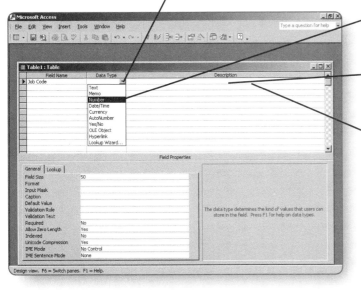

8. **Click** on the **desired data type**.

9. **Press** the **Tab key** to move to the Description column.

10. **Enter** a **description** of this field. Doing so is optional.

11. **Press** the **Tab key** to move back to the Field Name column.

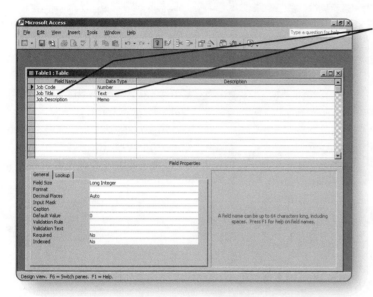

12. **Repeat Steps 5** through **11** until you have finished entering fields.

Setting a Primary Key

In each new table that you create, you'll want to set one field as the primary key. Access uses this key to relate this table's records to those in another table.

1. **Click** on the **field** that you want to set as the primary key. An arrow will appear in the field selector column.

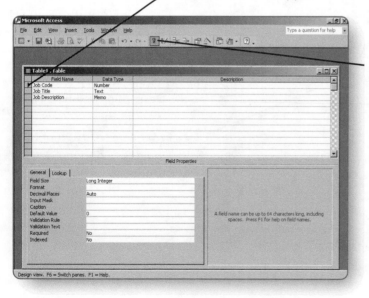

2. **Click** on the **Primary Key button**.

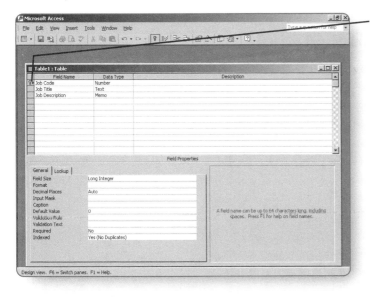

The field will be set as the primary key, indicated by a small key in the field selector column. The primary key is a toggle. To remove it, select the primary key field and click on the Primary Key button again.

Setting Format Properties

Access always sets each field with the default format for its data type. This format defines how the field displays in tables, forms, and reports. You might want to change this format to one of the other options. For example, a field with a Currency data type has a format of Currency by default. By changing the format, however, you can display this field in other ways, such as a percentage.

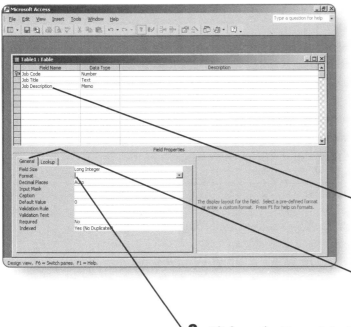

1. Click on the **field** whose format properties you want to set.

2. Click on the **General tab** in the Field Properties area.

3. Click on the **Format text box**. A down arrow will appear.

4. **Click** on the **down arrow** to display a list of possible formats.

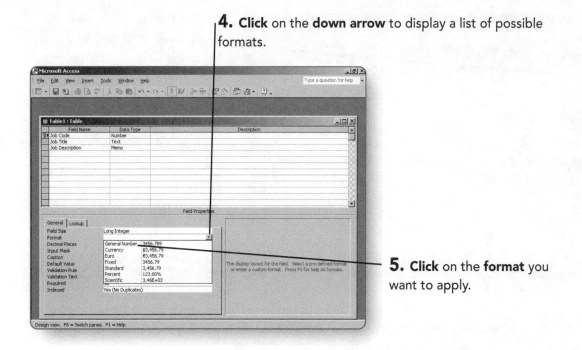

5. **Click** on the **format** you want to apply.

Setting Field Size Properties for Text Fields

The default field size for a field with a data type of Text is 50 characters. You can change this size to an amount anywhere in the range of 0 to 255 characters.

> ### CAUTION
> If you've already entered data in a table and you decrease the field size, you could lose some of your existing data if its length exceeds the new field size.

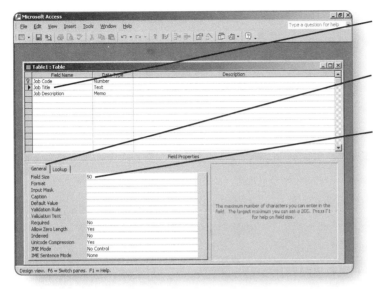

1. Click on the **field** whose field size you want to change.

2. Click on the **General tab** in the Field Properties area.

3. Enter the **new field size** in the Field Size text box.

Saving the Table

Once you finish creating your table, you'll want to save it.

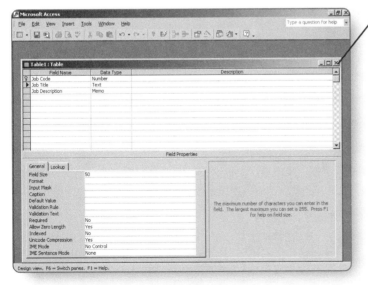

1. Click on the **Close button**. A dialog box will open, asking if you want to save the table.

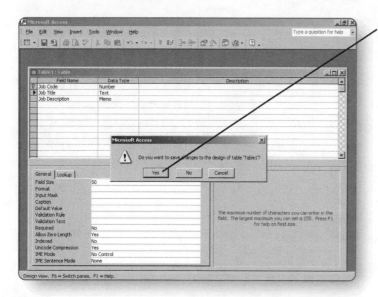

2. Click on **Yes**. The Save As dialog box will open.

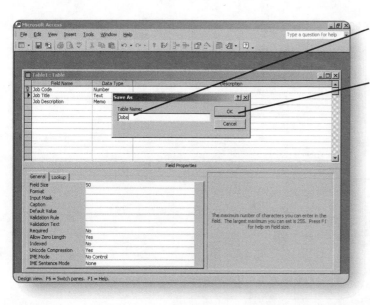

3. Enter a **name for your table** in the Table Name text box.

4. Click on **OK**. The main database window will appear again.

6

Modifying a Table

Once you create an Access table, you can easily modify it by adding, deleting, moving, or renaming table fields. In this chapter, you will learn how to:

- Open a table in Design view
- Insert, delete, rename, and move fields
- Change the data type

Opening a Table in Design View

To modify a table's design, you must open it in Design view.

1. Click on the **Tables button** in the main database window.

2. Click on the **table** you want to open. It will be highlighted.

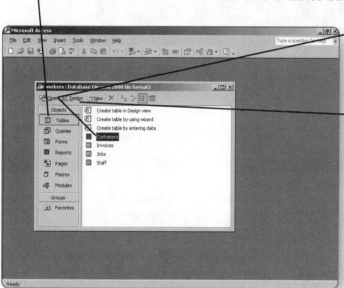

3. Click on the **Design button**. The table will open in Design view.

NOTE

You can also open a table in Design view directly from the Table Wizard by choosing the Modify the table design option button in the final wizard step.

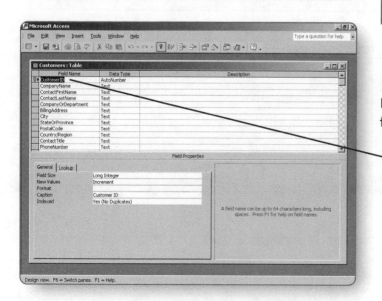

In Design view, you see each field's underlying structure:

- Field Name

● Data Type

● Description (if used)

● Field Properties

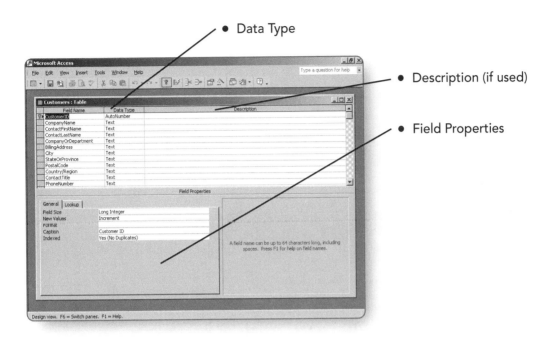

Inserting a Field

You can insert a field into an existing table.

1. Click on the **row** beneath which you want to add a field.

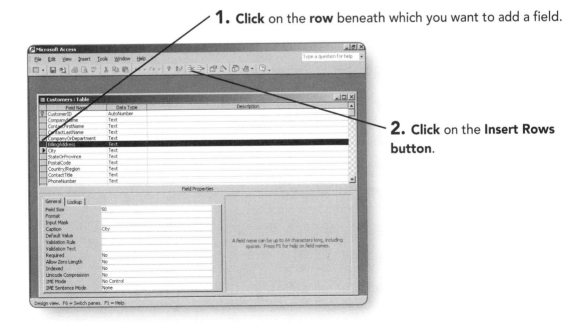

2. Click on the **Insert Rows button**.

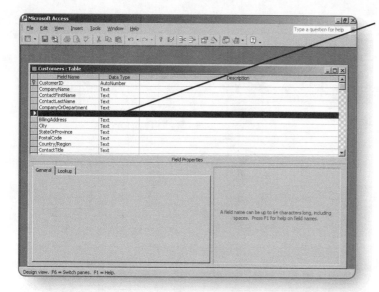

A blank row will be added.

Deleting a Field

You can easily delete a field from a table.

1. Click on **the field row** that you want to delete. An arrow will appear in the field selector column.

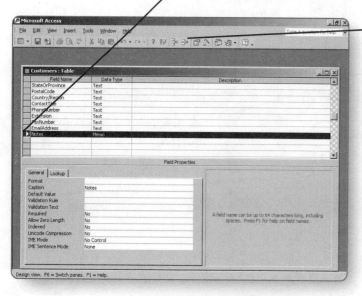

2. Click on the **Delete Rows button**. If you have entered any data into that field in the table, a dialog box will appear asking if you want to permanently delete the field and all its data.

3. **Click** on **Yes**. The field will be permanently deleted.

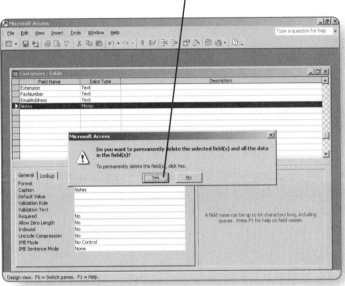

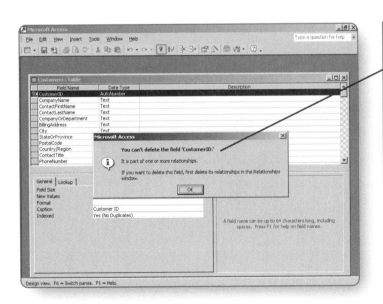

CAUTION

If this field is involved in a relationship between two tables, you won't be able to delete it. Remove the relationship, as you will learn in Chapter 7, "Managing Relationships between Tables," and then delete the field after removing the relationship.

TIP

To delete more than one field at a time, select the first field and, holding down the Ctrl key, continue selecting the remaining fields you want to delete.

Renaming a Field

You can also easily rename a field in an Access table. Remember that renaming a field can also affect reports, forms, and queries that contain the field. If you must rename the field in the table, you'll need to rename it in all other objects that contain it.

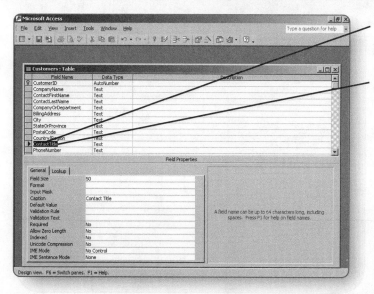

1. Select the **Field Name** that you want to rename.

2. Enter the **new name**.

Moving a Field

You can change the order of the fields in your table if you need to.

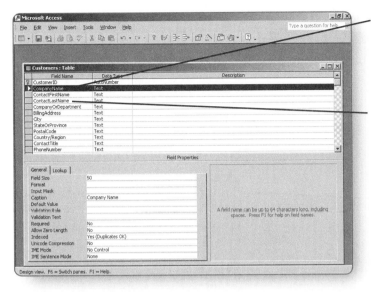

1. Click on the **field row** that you want to move. An arrow will appear in the field selector column.

2. Drag the **field** to a new location.

The field will be positioned in the new location.

Changing the Data Type

You can change the data type of existing table fields. For example, you might want to change a number field to a currency field.

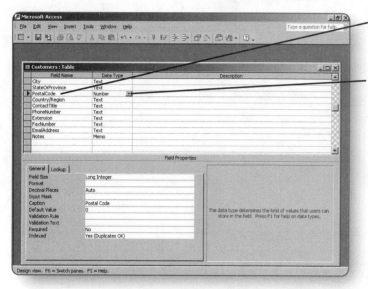

1. **Click** on the **field** whose data type you want to change.

2. **Click** on the **down arrow** to the right of the Data Type field whose data type you want to change. A menu will appear.

CAUTION

Remember that changing the data type of a field can restrict the types of entries you can make or even truncate existing entries. Also be sure that the data type you choose is compatible with the existing data. For example, if your existing field contains text and you change the data type to Number, Access displays a warning telling you that you will lose all your data if you make this data type change.

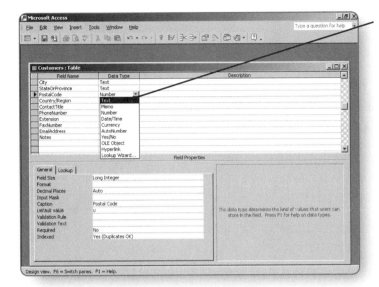

3. Click on the **new data type**. The new data type will become permanent when you save the table.

7

Managing Relationships between Tables

Good database design dictates that you separate data into multiple tables in all but the simplest databases. It's much easier to set up the tables and relationships between them before you begin entering data than to try to make changes after you have been using the database for a while.

In this chapter, you will learn how to:

- View a table's current relationships
- Create new relationships between tables
- Enforce referential integrity
- Remove relationships

Understanding Relationships

Relationships between tables enable you to link records in one table with the records in another, without necessarily having a one-to-one relationship. For example, you might have a Customers table and an Orders table. A single customer could have multiple orders. If you stored all the data in a single table, you would have to reenter a customer's contact information each time he placed an order. Instead, you can link the CustomerID field in the Customers table to the CustomerID field in the Orders table and then use the fields from the linked tables together in forms, queries, and other objects.

Viewing Table Relationships

If you are working with a database that you created using the Database Wizard, there are already relationships between some of your tables. You can view them by opening the Relationships window.

NOTE

If you created a blank database and added tables to it yourself, no relationships are set up yet. See the next section, "Creating Relationships," to create some.

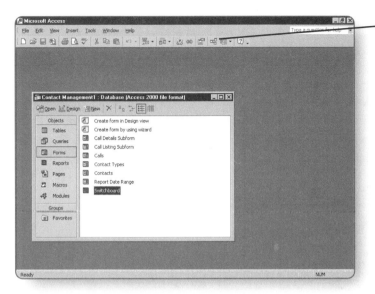

1. Click on the **Relationships button** on the toolbar. The Relationships window will open.

NOTE

If you see the Show Table dialog box at this point, there are no relationships yet. Skip to the section "Adding Tables to the Relationships Window," later in the chapter.

Each table appears in its own box. The primary key field for each table is bold. You can drag a box's title bar to reposition it.

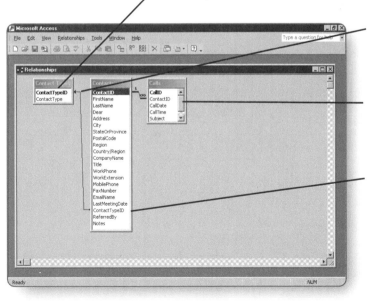

Lines indicate relationships between a field in one table and a field in another.

If all the field names do not fit, you can scroll through the list with the scroll bar.

You can also enlarge the box by dragging its border so that all the field names display at once, as shown here.

Creating Relationships

If you created your database using the Database Wizard, all the needed relationships are already in place. However, if you add a table to the database later, you might want to create a relationship between the new table and an existing one. If you started your database from scratch, you must create all the relationships yourself.

Adding Tables to the Relationships Window

The first time you open the Relationships window, if there are no existing relationships, you will be prompted to choose tables to add to the window. You can add all your tables to the window immediately, or just the few that you know you want to relate now. You can add more tables at any time.

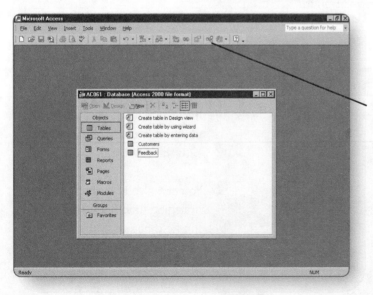

1. Click on the **Relationships button** if the Relationships window is not already open.

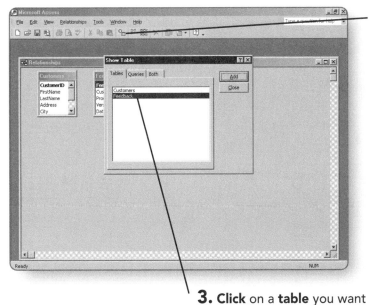

2. Click on the **Show Table button** if the Show Table dialog box does not automatically appear. The Show Table dialog box will open.

NOTE

If no relationships have yet been defined for this database, the Show Table dialog box appears automatically. If there are existing relationships or if there are already tables in the Relationships window, it does not.

3. Click on a **table** you want to display.

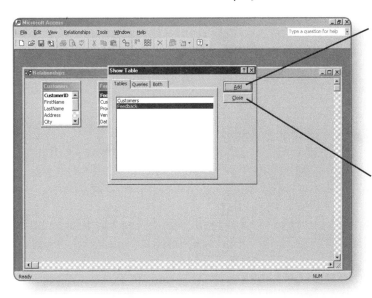

4. Click on **Add**. The table will appear in the Relationships window, behind the dialog box.

5. Repeat Steps 3 and 4 until all the tables you want to display have been added.

6. Click on **Close**. The Show Table dialog box will close.

Creating a Relationship

Creating a relationship between fields in two tables makes it possible to join their data in reports and queries and to cross-reference related data on a datasheet. The simplest type of relationship is one that has no special settings and no enforced referential integrity. (You'll learn about referential integrity later in this chapter.)

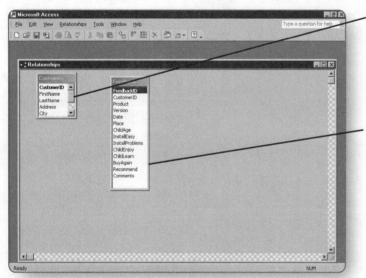

1a. **Drag** the **scroll bar** for each table so that the fields you want to relate are both visible.

OR

1b. **Drag** the **bottom border** of each table's box so that all the fields are visible at once.

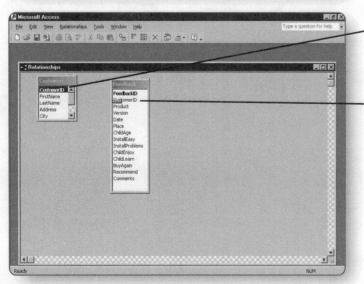

2. **Point** the **mouse pointer** at the field in one table that you want to relate to another.

3. **Hold** down the **left mouse button** and drag to the field in the second table. The mouse pointer will look like a small bar.

4. **Release** the **mouse button**. The Edit Relationships dialog box will appear.

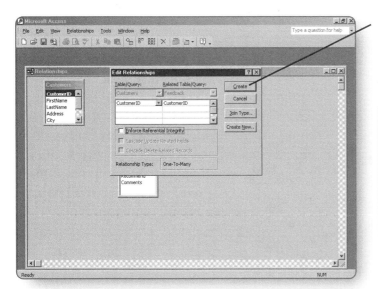

5. Click on **Create**. The relationship will be created, and a line will appear joining the two fields.

NOTE

In the preceding steps you did not enforce referential integrity. See the following section to learn about that feature.

Understanding Referential Integrity

Referential integrity keeps you from making data-entry mistakes. It says, essentially, that all the information in the linked fields should match and provides rules to apply when it does not.

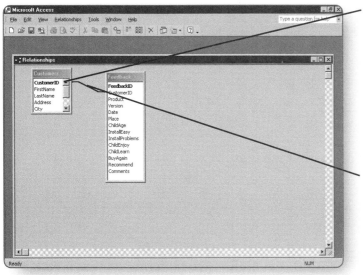

Most relationships are one-to-many. The CustomerID field in the Customers table, for example, is unique for each record. The Feedback table, however, can contain many records with the same CustomerID.

In a normal relationship, it is not important which table is the "one" and which is the "many." Therefore, such relationships display as a plain line.

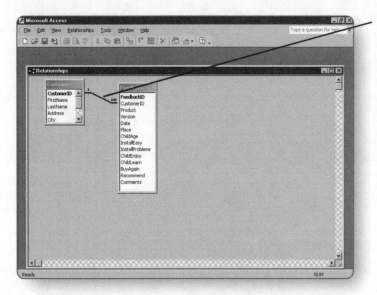

However, when you enforce referential integrity, no entries on the "many" side will be allowed that do not already exist on the "one" side, so it becomes important which side is which. Therefore, such relationship lines have 1 and ∞ signs to show which side is the "one" and which is the "many."

Enforcing Referential Integrity for a Relationship

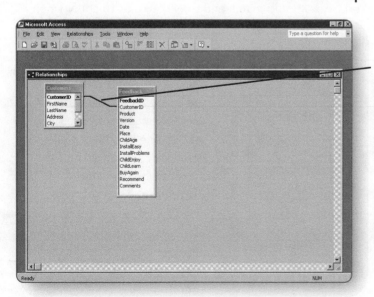

1. Double-click on the **relationship line** between two tables. The Edit Relationships dialog box will open.

2. Click on the **Enforce Referential Integrity check box**. A check mark will appear in it, and two additional check boxes will become available.

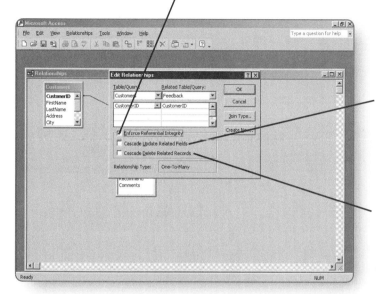

3. Mark either or **both** of the **additional check boxes** as desired:

Click on **Cascade Update Related Fields** to automatically change entries on the "many" side if an entry changes on the "one" side.

Click on **Cascade Delete Related Fields** to automatically delete entire records from the table on the "many" side if the related entry in the table on the "one" side is deleted.

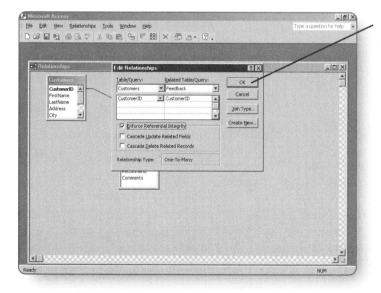

4. Click on **OK**. The line joining the fields will appear with a 1 at one end and an ∞ at the other.

Removing a Relationship

If you decide not to have a relationship between two tables, you can remove the relationship line.

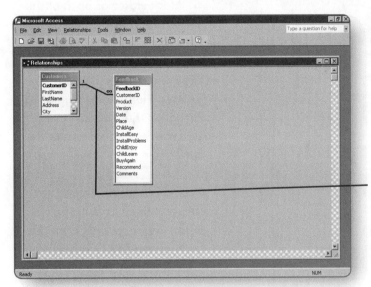

1. Click on the **relationship line**.

2. Press the **Delete** key. A confirmation box will appear.

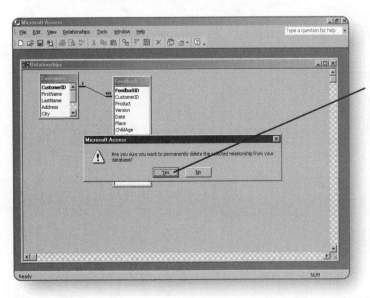

3. Click on **Yes**. The relationship line will be removed.

TIP

Another way to remove all relationships from a table is to remove the table itself from the Relationships window. To do so, click the table box's title bar and press the Delete key.

Closing the Relationships Window

When you are finished working with relationships, you can close the Relationships window.

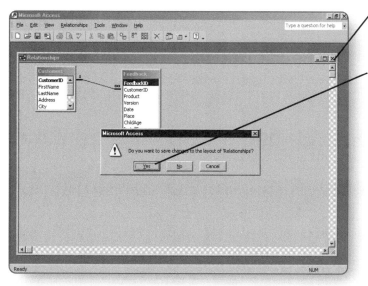

1. **Click** on the **Close** button. A confirmation box will appear.

2. **Click** on **Yes**. The Relationships window will close.

Part II Review Questions

1. How do you change the name of a field during the Table Wizard's table creation process? *See "Renaming Fields" in Chapter 4*

2. What happens if you allow the Table Wizard to set a primary key for you? *See "Naming the Table and Setting a Key" in Chapter 4*

3. Can relationships between tables be set from the Table Wizard? *See "Setting Table Relationships" in Chapter 4*

4. When Access creates a new table in Datasheet view, what are the default names of the fields? *See "Creating a Table in Datasheet View" in Chapter 5*

5. Which of the following is not a valid field type in Table Design view: OLE Object, Memo, Text, or Calculated? *See "Creating a Table in Design View" in Chapter 5*

6. How do you specify which field should be unique for each record? *See "Setting a Primary Key" in Chapter 5*

7. How do you add a new field to an existing table? *See "Inserting a Field" in Chapter 6*

8. Where do you change the data type of a table field? *See "Changing the Data Type" in Chapter 6*

9. Why might you want to create a relationship between fields in different tables? *See "Understanding Relationships" in Chapter 7*

10. What is referential integrity? *See "Understanding Referential Integrity" in Chapter 7*

PART III

Entering, Editing, and Viewing Data

8

Entering Data

Access offers two ways to enter data into tables. You can enter new data while existing data is in view, or you can hide the existing data while you enter new data. In this chapter, you will learn how to:

- Open a table in Datasheet view
- Use Edit mode to enter data
- Use Data Entry mode to enter data

Opening a Table in Datasheet View

To enter data in a table, you need to open it in Datasheet view.

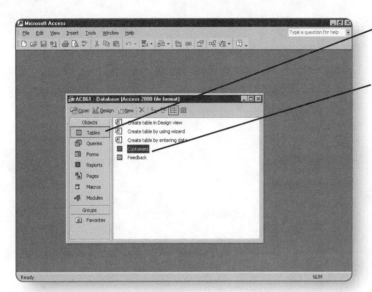

1. **Click** on the **Tables button** in the main database window.

2. **Double-click** on the **table** that you want to open. It will open in Datasheet view.

NOTE

You can also open a table in Datasheet view directly from the Table Wizard by choosing the Enter data directly into the table option button in the final wizard step.

Datasheet view looks similar to a spreadsheet such as those you see in Excel. It uses a row and column format to display table data in a series of fields.

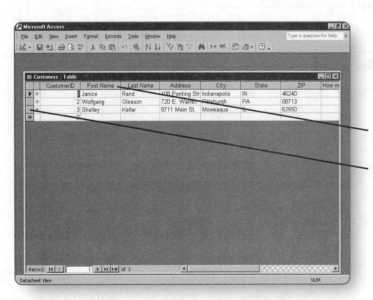

Each column is a field.

Each row is a record.

Navigating in Datasheet View

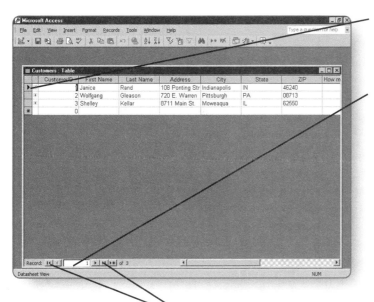

Access identifies the current record with an arrow in the record selector column.

The record number box at the bottom of the screen also displays the current record number.

The navigation buttons to the left and right of this box help you navigate the table. Using these buttons, you can move to the first, preceding, next, or last record.

You can also use the mouse to navigate the datasheet or to select the field you want, or you can use shortcut key combinations like those shown in the following table.

Key	Purpose
Enter or Tab	Navigates to the next field.
Shift+Tab	Navigates to the preceding field.
Page Up	Navigates up one screen.
Page Down	Navigates down one screen.

See Appendix C, "Using Keyboard Shortcuts," for a more detailed list.

Using Edit Mode to Enter Data

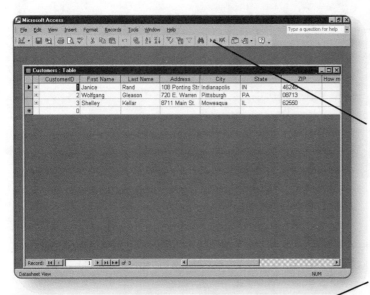

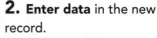

Edit mode is the normal mode for a datasheet. It displays all the current records and enables you to add new ones at the bottom of the list.

1. **Click** on the **New Record** button. A blank record will appear at the bottom of the table.

2. **Enter data** in the new record.

3. **Tab** to the **next blank record** when you finish entering data in the first.

4. Repeat Steps 2 and **3** until you finish adding data.

TIP

You can also click on the New Record button to the right of the navigation buttons to add a new record.

NOTE

Access automatically enters the next consecutive number in an AutoNumber field once you tab out of that field.

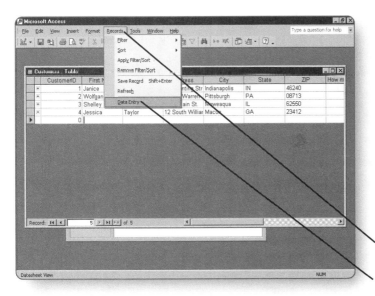

Using Data Entry Mode to Enter Data

You can also use Data Entry mode to enter data into a datasheet. Data Entry mode displays a blank table and temporarily hides all previously entered records from view.

1. Click on **Records**.

2. Click on **Data Entry**. Data Entry mode will be activated.

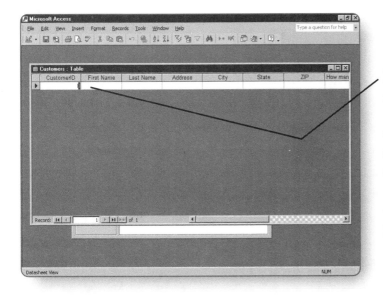

3. Enter data in the new record.

4. Tab to the **next blank record** when you finish entering data in the first.

5. Repeat Steps 3 and **4** until you finish adding data.

Exiting Data Entry Mode

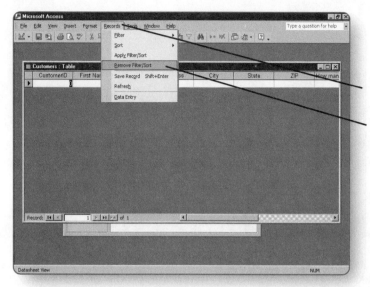

When you finish entering data, you can deactivate Data Entry mode.

1. **Click** on **Records**.

2. **Click** on **Remove Filter/Sort**.

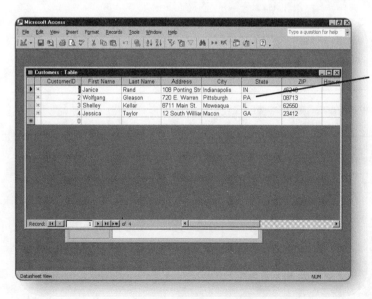

The hidden records will appear again.

9

Editing Data

You can edit and modify data in Access with the security of knowing that you can undo your last edit. Access also includes a powerful find and replace feature that lets you quickly update large amounts of data. In this chapter, you will learn how to:

- Modify data
- Undo edits
- Replace data
- Delete records

Modifying Data

You can modify an existing table entry in Datasheet view by replacing all or part of the data.

Modifying the Entire Field Contents

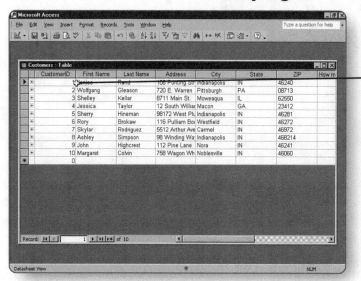

You can replace the entire contents of the selected field.

1. **Place** the **mouse pointer** on the left side of the field. A large white plus sign will appear.

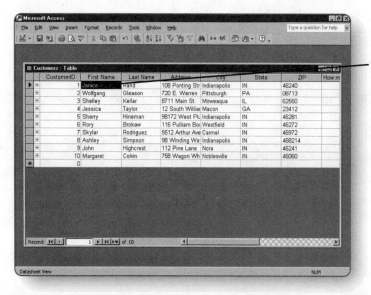

2. **Click** on the **field**. The entire field will be highlighted.

3. **Replace** the **existing field data** with new data.

Modifying Partial Field Contents

You can replace parts—such as individual words—of selected field contents.

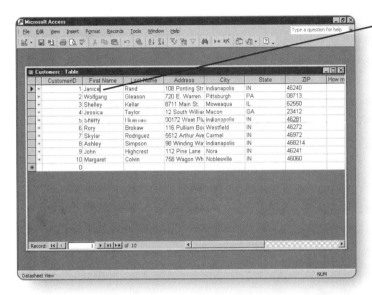

1. Click on the **field** whose data you want to modify. The I-beam pointer will appear.

2. Replace the **desired data** with new information.

Undoing Edits

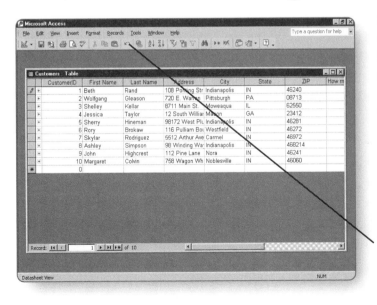

If you make a mistake while editing data, you can often undo it. The Undo feature lets you undo the last edit you made. Depending on your last action, the label for the Undo button might display Undo Typing, Undo Current Field/Record, or Undo Saved Record. If there is nothing to undo, the button label will display Can't Undo.

To use the Undo feature, click on the Undo button on the tool-bar. The last edit will be undone.

Replacing Data

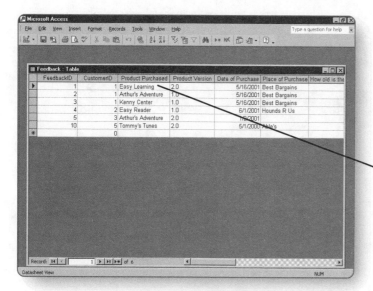

Using the Replace feature, you can quickly search for and replace specific data in a table that is open in Datasheet view. This is particularly useful with tables that contain hundreds or even thousands of records.

1. Click on a **field** in the column in which you want to replace data.

2. Click on **Edit**.

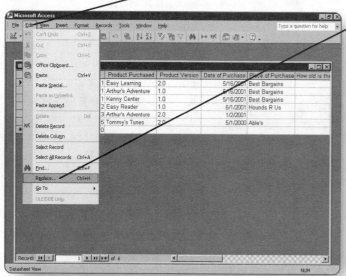

3. Click on **Replace**. The Find and Replace dialog box will open with the Replace tab selected.

TIP

If the Replace menu option doesn't appear, click on the double down arrows at the bottom of the Edit menu. Additional menu options will be displayed.

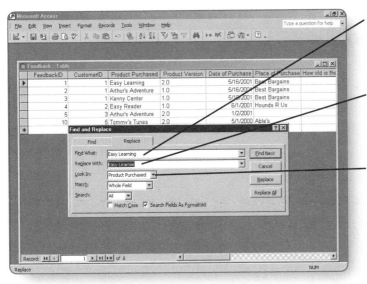

4. Enter the **text** that you want to replace in the Find What text box.

5. Enter the **text** that you want to use as a replacement in the Replace With text box.

6. Click on the **down arrow** to the right of the Look In list box. A drop-down list will appear.

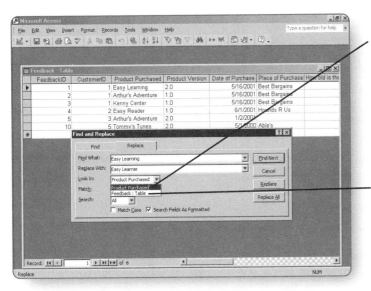

7a. Click on the **default field name** in order to search only the field you selected in Step 1. The default field name will appear in the Look In list box.

OR

7b. Select the **table name** to replace fields throughout the entire table.

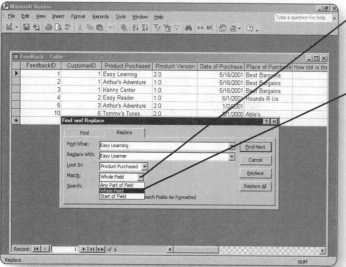

8. Click on the **down arrow** to the right of the Match list box. A drop-down list will appear.

9. Click on **one** of the following **options**:

- Select Any Part of Field to locate entries that match any portion of your search criteria.

- Select Whole Field to locate only those entries that exactly match your search criteria.

- Select Start of Field to locate only those entries that match the initial letters of your search criteria.

The option you select will appear in the Match list box.

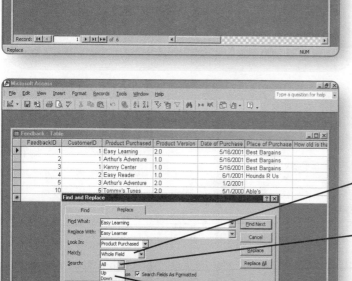

10. Click on the **down arrow** to the right of the Search list box. A drop-down list will appear.

11. Click on **one** of the following **options**:

- Choose Up to search only the records prior to the currently selected record.

- Choose Down to search only the records after the currently selected record.

- Choose All to search the entire table for your specified criteria.

NOTE
The record in which you clicked to select the search field in Step 1 is the currently selected record.

12. **Click** on the **Match Case check box** to locate only those entries that exactly match the case in your search criteria.

13. **Click** on the **Search Fields As Formatted check box** to locate only fields that match the exact formatting of the search criteria.

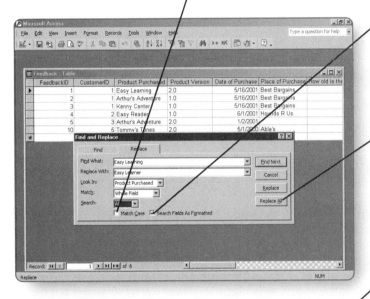

14. **Click** on the **Replace All button** to replace all instances of the entered text. A confirmation box will appear.

15. **Click** on **Yes**. The replacements will be made.

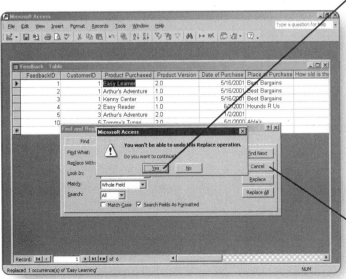

TIP
You can also click on the Find Next button to find the next match and then click on Replace to replace the text if you want to view each match before replacing it.

16. **Click** on **Cancel** to exit the Find and Replace dialog box.

Deleting Records

You can delete records from Access tables.

1. Click on the **record selector column** of the record you want to delete. The row will be highlighted.

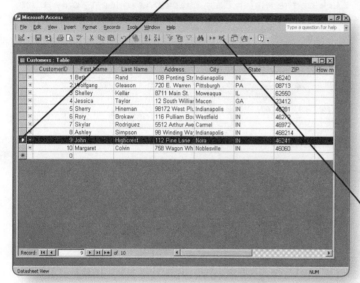

TIP

To select more than one contiguous record for deletion, hold down the Shift key and click on another record. That record, and all records in between, will be highlighted.

2a. Click on the **Delete Record button**

OR

2b. Press the **Delete** key on the keyboard. A warning message box will appear.

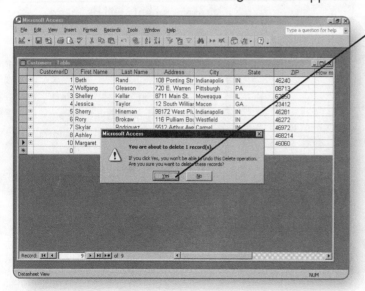

3. Click on **Yes** to permanently delete the record.

CAUTION

You might not be able to delete a record if a field in the table is related to a field in another table and referential integrity has been enforced (see Chapter 7, "Managing Relationships between Tables").

10

Changing the Datasheet Layout

In Datasheet view, you can make many layout modifications to display the datasheet in the format that's most convenient for you. In this chapter, you'll learn how to:

- Resize datasheet columns and rows
- Freeze and unfreeze columns
- Hide and unhide columns
- Rename columns
- View subdatasheets

Resizing Datasheet Columns

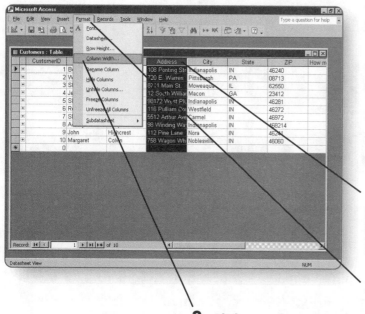

In Datasheet view, you can resize the width of individual columns—for example, to view the complete contents of a long field. This affects only the on-screen appearance of the individual datasheet; it does not affect reports and forms based on the datasheet table.

1. **Click** on the **column indicator button** of the column you want to resize. It will be highlighted.

2. **Click** on **Format**.

3. **Click** on **Column Width**. The Column Width dialog box will open.

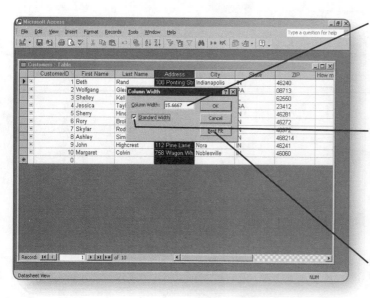

4a. **Enter** the **exact column width** in the Column Width text box.

OR

4b. **Click** on the **Standard Width check box**. The column width will default to approximately 15 characters.

OR

4c. **Click** on the **Best Fit button**. The column width will adjust to display the headings and all field values.

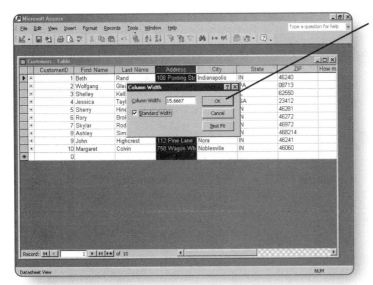

5. Click on **OK** if the dialog box didn't automatically close when you clicked on the Best Fit button.

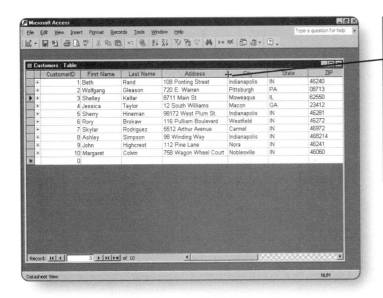

TIP

You can also automatically set the best fit by double-clicking on the black arrow that appears when you place the mouse pointer to the right of a column header.

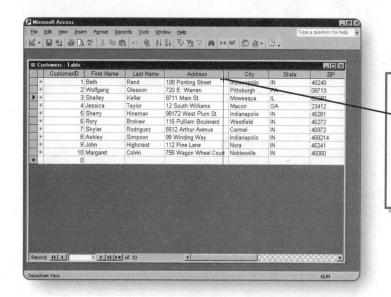

TIP

To manually adjust the column width, drag the black arrow to the left or right to reposition the column grid.

Resizing Datasheet Rows

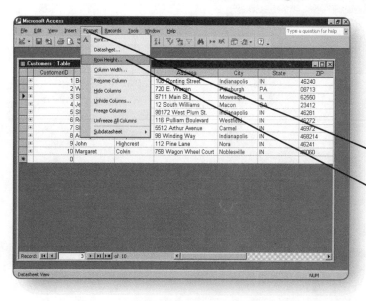

You can resize row height in Datasheet view. Unlike with columns, rows are resized as a whole. You cannot make one row a different height than the others.

1. Click on **Format**.

2. Click on **Row Height**. The Row Height dialog box will open.

3a. **Enter** the **exact row height** in the Row Height text box.

OR

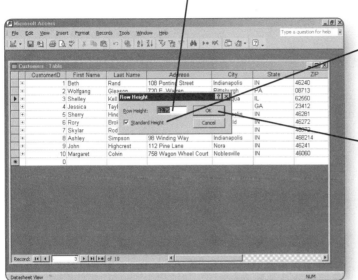

3b. **Click** on the **Standard Height check box**. The row height will default to approximately 12.75 points.

4. **Click** on **OK**.

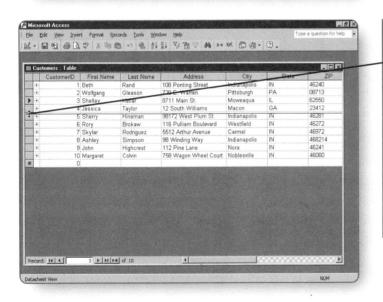

TIP

To manually adjust the row height, place the mouse pointer next to the record locator column; when it turns into an up-down arrow, resize the row as desired. This changes all rows at once, regardless of which row you drag.

Freezing and Unfreezing Columns

If you have many columns (fields) in your table, you won't be able to view the far-left columns if you scroll to the right. If you want a column or columns to always be visible, you can freeze them. For example, in a table that contains employee information, you might always want to see employee names as you scroll across columns to view their information.

Freezing Columns

You can freeze one or more columns.

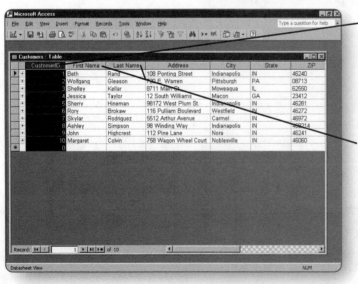

1. **Click** on the **column header** of the first column you want to freeze.

2. (Optional) **Hold down Shift** and **click on other column headers** if you want to freeze more than one column.

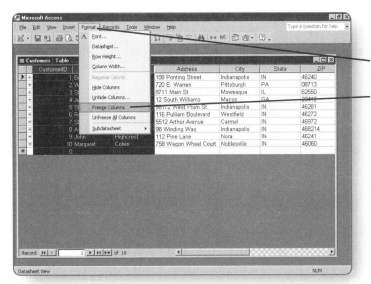

3. Click on **Format**.

4. Click on **Freeze Columns**.

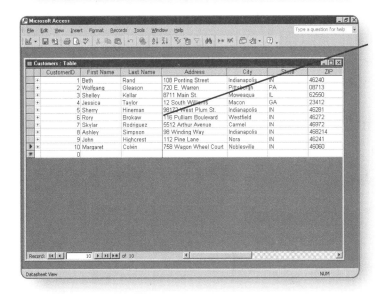

A vertical black line will appear in the grid to the right of the last frozen column.

Unfreezing Columns

If you no longer want to have the frozen columns always visible, you can unfreeze them.

1. Click on **Format**.

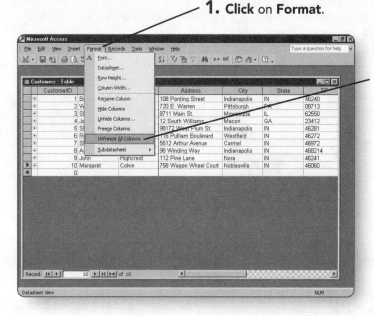

2. Click on **Unfreeze All Columns**.

Hiding and Unhiding Columns

Sometimes you might want to focus on only a few fields in your table. In a large table, it can be confusing to view many fields, some of which are important to the table structure but convey no necessary information. ID and AutoNumber fields are examples of these types of fields.

Hiding Columns

You can temporarily hide any columns that you don't want to view.

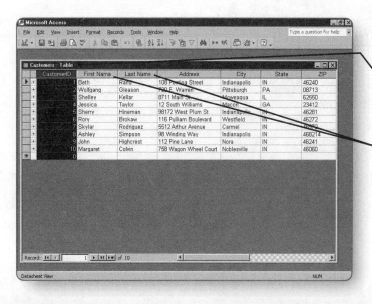

1. Click on the **column header** of the column you want to hide.

2. (Optional) **Hold down Shift** and **click** on **other columns** if you want to hide more than one column.

3. Click on **Format**. The Format menu will appear.

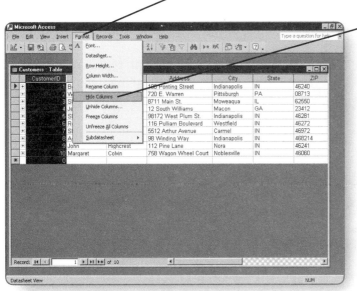

4. Click on **Hide Columns**. The columns will disappear from view, but they aren't deleted.

Unhiding Columns

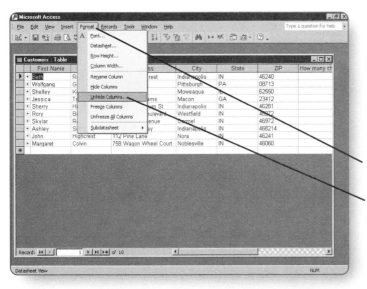

You'll use the Unhide Columns dialog box to select the columns you want to unhide. A check mark appears in the check boxes of all visible columns; hidden columns have no check mark.

1. Click on **Format**.

2. Click on **Unhide Columns**. The Unhide Columns dialog box will open.

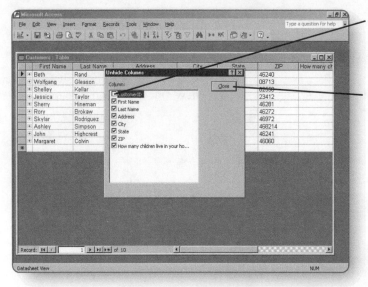

3. **Click** on the **check boxes** next to the columns that you want to unhide.

4. **Click** on **Close**. The columns will appear again.

Renaming Columns

You can rename a field column directly in Datasheet view, rather than having to go into Table Design view.

1. **Click** on the **column header** of the column that you want to rename.

2. **Click** on **Format**.

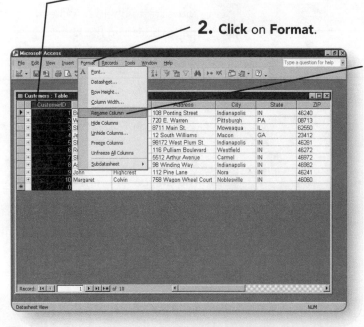

3. **Click** on **Rename Column**. The column header name will be selected.

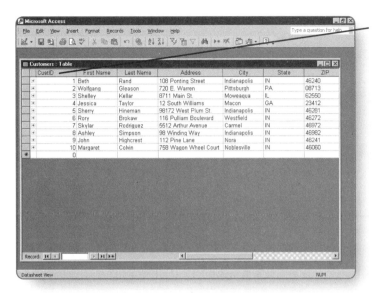

4. Type a **new column name** and **press Enter**. When you save the table, the new column (field) name will be permanent.

NOTE

You can't rename more than one column at a time.

Working with Subdatasheets

In Datasheet view, you can view the data of other related tables. For example, if you have a Customers table that includes a one-to-many relationship with an Orders table, each customer has probably placed more than one order. Using subdatasheets, you can view a list of orders for each customer from within the Customers table.

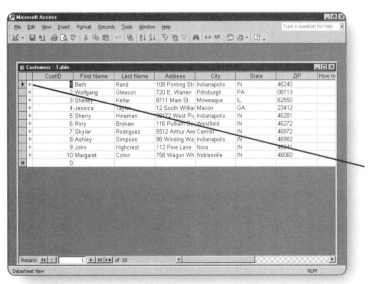

Viewing a Subdatasheet

From Datasheet view, you can easily view the matching records from a related table.

1. Click on the **plus sign** next to a record.

The subdatasheet for the related table will appear.

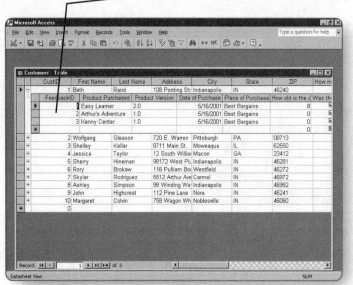

TIP

You can view all the sub-datasheets at once for the entire table by choosing Format, Subdatasheet, Expand All. To collapse all subdatasheets at once, choose Format, Sub-datasheet, Collapse All.

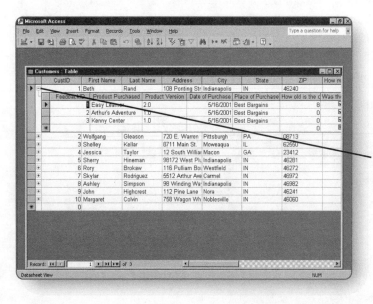

Closing a Subdatasheet

You can collapse the sub-datasheet when you finish viewing it.

1. Click on the **minus sign** next to the field. The subdatasheet will collapse.

Part III Review Questions

1. Which view do you use to enter data in a table? *See "Opening a Table in Datasheet View" in Chapter 8*

2. What is the difference between Edit mode and Data Entry mode? *See "Using Edit Mode to Enter Data" and "Using Data Entry Mode to Enter Data" in Chapter 8*

3. How can you correct a mistake you make editing a table? *See "Undoing Edits" in Chapter 9*

4. How can you replace all instances of a word or phrase across many records? *See "Replacing Data" in Chapter 9*

5. What is a quick way to resize a column so that the content exactly fits in the Datasheet view? *See "Resizing Datasheet Columns" in Chapter 10*

6. Is it possible to resize a single row in a datasheet without resizing the other rows? *See "Resizing Datasheet Rows" in Chapter 10*

7. What command makes a column perpetually visible as you scroll from left to right? *See "Freezing and Unfreezing Columns" in Chapter 10*

8. How can you temporarily remove certain columns from Datasheet view? *See "Hiding and Unhiding Columns" in Chapter 10*

9. How do you change the name of a field in Datasheet view? *See "Renaming Columns" in Chapter 10*

10. What is a subdatasheet, and what does it display? *See "Viewing a Subdatasheet" in Chapter 10*

PART IV

Finding Data

11

Sorting, Filtering, and Finding Data

Access includes several features that help you locate, organize, and analyze specific information in your tables while in Datasheet view. In this chapter, you'll learn how to:

- Sort data
- Filter data
- Find data

Sorting Data

By default, records in a table appear in the order in which they were entered. You can re-sort them based on any field, however, in ascending or descending order.

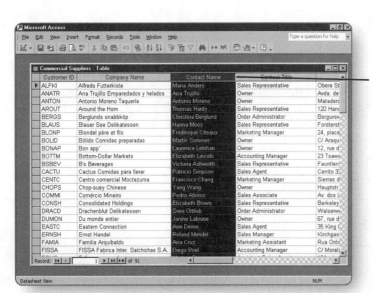

NOTE

When you perform a sort, the new order is not permanent; when you close the datasheet and reopen it, the records will appear in their original order.

1. Click on the **field or fields** on which you want to sort.

TIP

To sort by more than one field, click on the first field and then press and hold the Shift key as you click on additional fields. Regardless of which order you select them in, Access considers the far-left field to be the first field in the sort. Additional selected fields are used only to resolve a tie if two records have the same value in the first sort field.

2a. **Click** on the **Sort Ascending button** on the toolbar.

OR

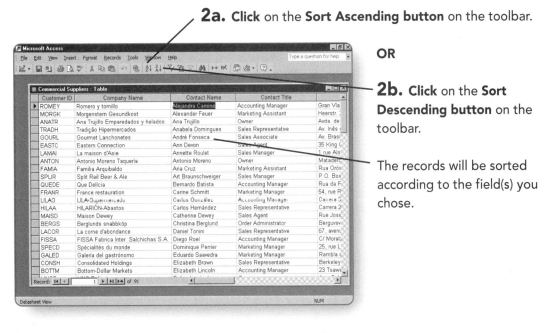

2b. **Click** on the **Sort Descending button** on the toolbar.

The records will be sorted according to the field(s) you chose.

Removing a Sort

After applying a sort, you can remove it and restore the default order of the table data.

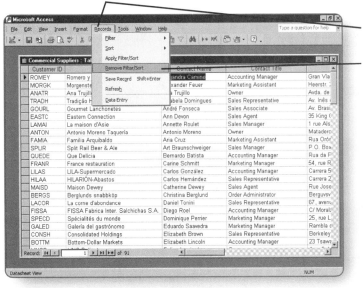

1. **Click** on **Records**.

2. **Click** on **Remove Filter/Sort**. The default order of the table data will be restored to the original order.

Filtering Data

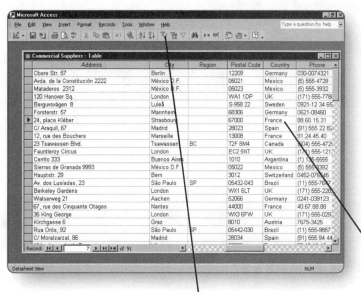

Filter by Selection lets you select specific data in a table that is open in Datasheet view and then quickly apply a basic filter. For example, if you want to view only records for customers located in France, you could click on any field containing the word "France" and apply Filter by Selection to view these records.

1. **Click** on a **field** that contains the data on which you want to filter.

2. **Click** on the **Filter by Selection button**.

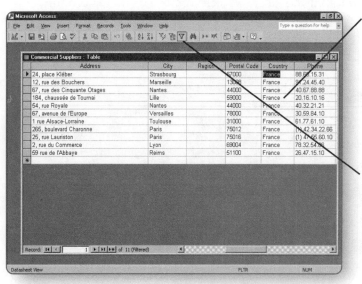

Only the records that contain this data are displayed. Access hides all other records.

To remove the filter, click on the Remove Filter button. The Remove Filter button will become the Apply Filter button. Click on it again to reapply your last filter.

Filtering by Form

The Filter by Form feature lets you filter based on more than one criterion. Using this feature, you can filter based on both AND and OR criteria. If you specify AND criteria, Access will display only those records that meet all the specified criteria.

For example, if you filter on customers located in San Francisco *and* customers in the real estate industry, only records with both criteria will be displayed. If you filter on customers in San Francisco *or* customers in the real estate industry, records that meet either condition will be displayed.

1. **Click** on the **Filter by Form button**. The Filter by Form window will appear with the Look for tab active.

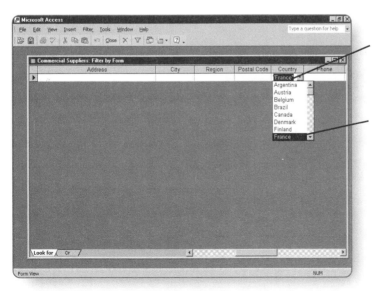

2. **Click** on the **field** on which you want to filter. A drop-down list will open for that field.

3. **Click** on the **filter criterion** that you want to use from the drop-down list.

4. **Repeat Steps 2** and **3** until you select all desired AND criteria.

5. Click on the **Or tab** if you want to specify OR criteria.

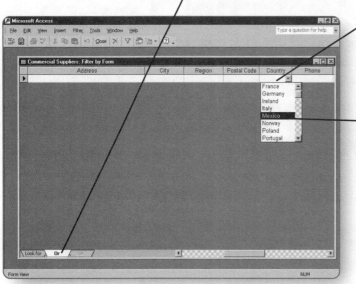

6. Click on another **field** on which you want to filter. A drop-down list will appear for the selected field.

7. Click on the **filter criterion** that you want to use from the drop-down list.

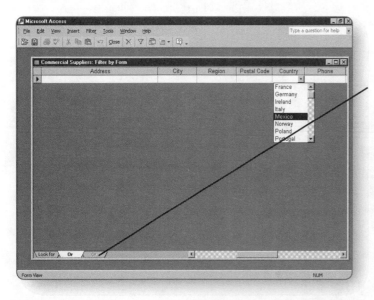

8. Click on the **next Or tab** if you want to specify another OR criterion.

9. Repeat Steps 6 through **8** until you finish specifying OR criteria.

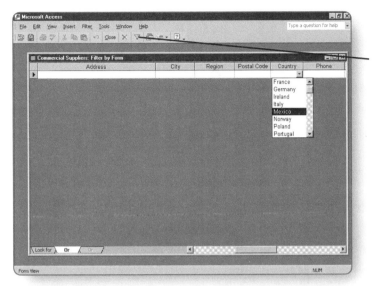

10. **Click** on the **Apply Filter button**.

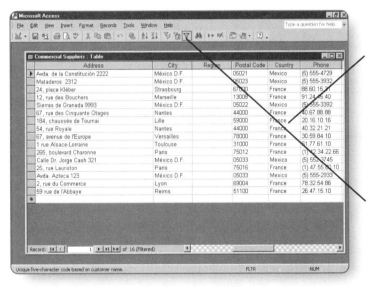

The filter results will appear.

Once you've viewed the filter results, click on the Remove Filter button to remove the filter and restore the original data.

Saving a Filter by Form

While you are in the Filter by Form window, you can save filter by form results as a query.

NOTE

A *query* is a set of saved rules by which a table (or multiple tables) should be arranged, sorted, filtered, and displayed. Queries are covered in more detail in Chapters 12 through 14.

1. Click on the **Save As Query button**. The Save As Query dialog box will open.

2. Enter a **name** in the Query Name text box.

3. Click on **OK**.

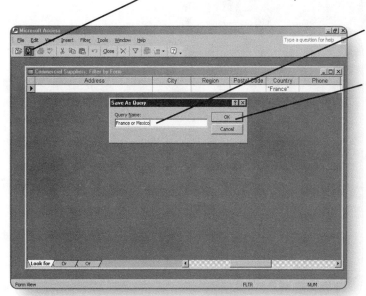

TIP

When you want to view these filter results again, click on Queries in the main database window and select the query by name.

Finding Data

Using the Find feature, you can quickly search for specific data in a table that is open in Datasheet view. This is particularly useful with tables that contain hundreds or even thousands of records.

NOTE

The Find feature is similar to the Replace feature that you learned about in Chapter 9, "Editing Data."

1. Click on the **field** in which you want to search.

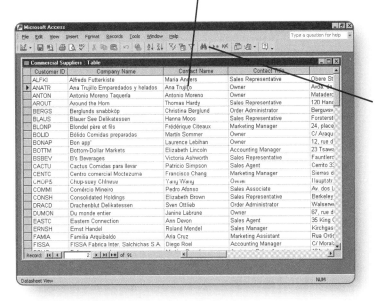

2. Click on the **Find button**. The Find and Replace dialog box will open with the Find tab selected.

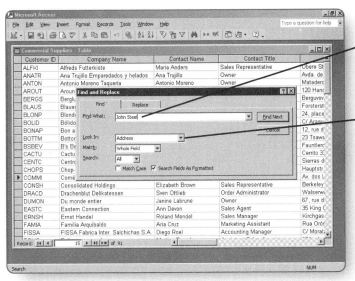

3. Enter the **word or words** on which you want to search in the Find What text box.

4. Click on the **down arrow** to the right of the Look In list box. A menu will appear.

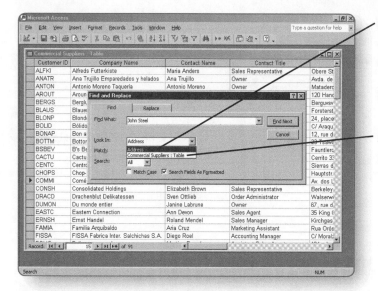

5a. **Click** on the **default field name** in order to search only the field you selected in Step 1.

OR

5b. **Click** on the **table name** to search the entire table.

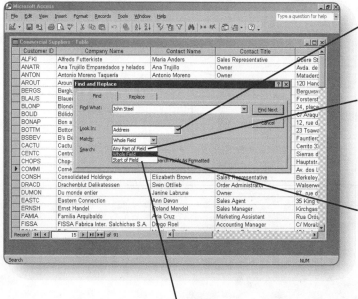

6. **Click** on the **down arrow** to the right of the Match list box. A menu will appear.

7a. **Click** on **Any Part of Field** to locate entries that match any portion of your search criteria.

OR

7b. **Click** on **Whole Field** to locate only those entries that exactly match your search criteria.

OR

7c. **Click** on **Start of Field** to locate only those entries that match the initial letters of your search criteria.

TIP

Searching for only the start of the field or parts of fields is useful when you can't remember the exact entry you're looking for.

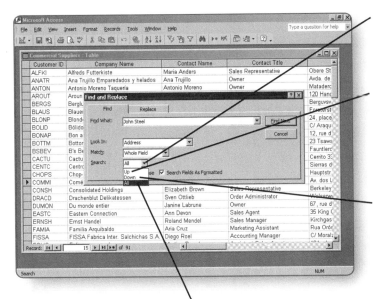

8. **Click** on the **down arrow** to the right of the Search list box. A menu will appear.

9a. **Click** on **Up** to search only the records prior to the currently selected record.

OR

9b. **Click** on **Down** to search only the records after the currently selected record.

OR

9c. **Click** on **All** to search the entire table for your specified criteria.

NOTE

The currently selected record is the record in which you clicked to select the search field in Step 1.

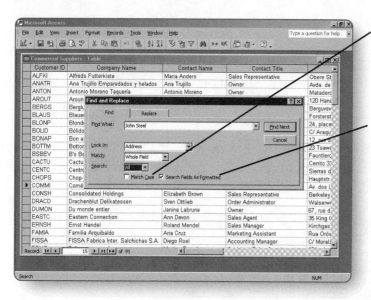

10. Click on the **Match Case check box** to locate only those entries that exactly match the case in your search criteria.

11. Click on the **Search Fields As Formatted check box** to locate only fields that match the exact formatting of the search criteria.

NOTE

Searching Fields As Formatted is useful if you want to search for only exact date formatting. For example, entering 10/15/00 would not match with the entry October 15, 2000 if this check box were selected.

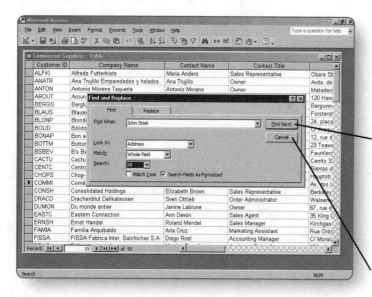

12. Click on the **Find Next button** to display the next match.

13. Repeat Step 12 until you view all desired matches.

14. Click on **Cancel** to exit the Find and Replace dialog box.

12

Using the Simple Query Wizard

The Simple Query Wizard guides you through the creation of a basic query that extracts specific fields from tables or other queries. In this chapter, you'll learn how to:

- Start the Simple Query Wizard
- Select fields
- Choose a detail or summary query
- Finish the query

Starting the Simple Query Wizard

A *query* extracts and arranges information from one or more tables in a manner that you specify. A good way to start learning about queries is to create one with the Simple Query Wizard. It creates a *select query*, a basic kind of query that displays certain fields from a table in a datasheet-like view. You might use one, for example, to extract names and phone numbers from a table that included more complete contact information for a list of people.

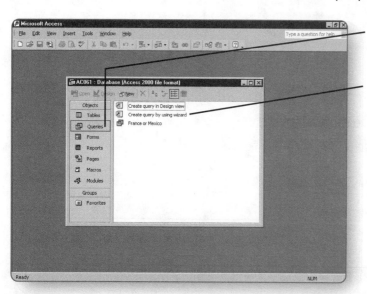

1. **Click** on the **Queries button** in the main database window.

2. **Double-click** on **Create query by using wizard** within the database window. The Simple Query Wizard will open.

Selecting Fields

In the next step, you choose the specific fields to include in your query and indicate the table or other query in which they are located.

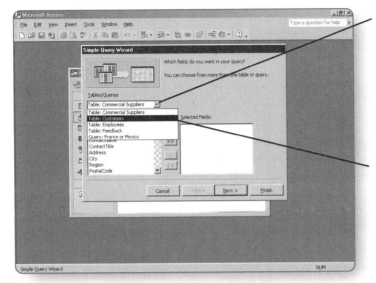

1. **Click** on the **down arrow** to the right of the Tables/Queries box. A menu will appear.

2. **Click on the table or query** from which you want to select your query field. A list of the fields for that table/query will appear.

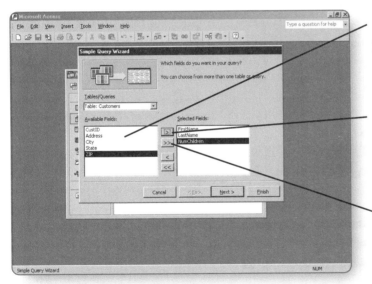

3. **Choose** the **first field that you want** to include in your query from the Available Fields list.

4. **Click** on the **right arrow button**. The field will move to the Selected Fields list.

TIP

You can quickly include all available fields by clicking on the double right arrow button.

5. **Repeat Steps 1** through **3** until you select all fields to include in the query.

You can include fields from multiple tables/queries as long as there is a relationship between them (see Chapter 7, "Managing Relationships between Tables").

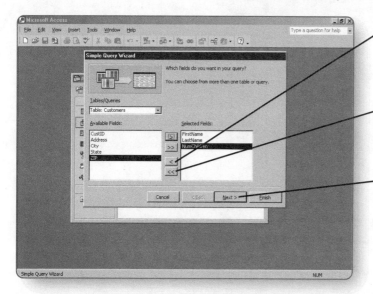

Click on the left arrow button to remove the selected field from the query.

Click on the double left arrow button to remove all fields from your query.

6. **Click** on **Next**. The Simple Query Wizard will continue to the next step.

Choosing a Detail or Summary Query

If you include number fields in your query, you can display either detailed or summary information. If you did not choose any fields of the Number type, skip to the section "Finishing the Query," later in this chapter.

Creating a Detail Query

A detail query includes all fields in all records. It is the default.

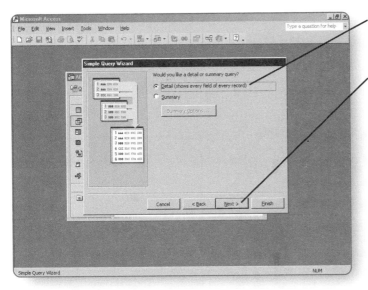

1. Click on the **Detail** option button.

2. Click on **Next** to continue.

Creating a Summary Query

A summary query lets you summarize information in your select query. Through the Summary Options dialog box, you can specify up to four different summary options for each numeric field in your query. These options include the ability to summarize a field as well as to display its average, minimum, or maximum.

1. Click on the **Summary** option button. The Summary Options button will become active.

2. Click on the **Summary Options** button. The Summary Options dialog box will open.

3. Click on the **check box** for each field and summary option combination you want to include in your query.

4. Click on the **Count records in {table name} check box** to display the record count in the query.

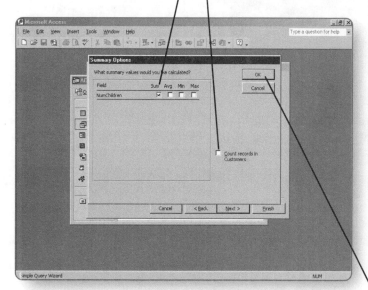

NOTE

In this example, the check box is named Count records in Customers because the query is based on the Customers table. The dialog box will substitute the name of whatever table you actually use to create your query.

5. Click on **OK** to return to the Simple Query Wizard.

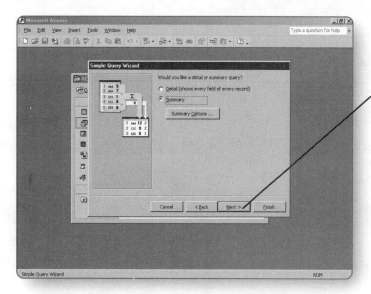

6. Click on **Next** to continue to the next step.

Finishing the Query

In the Simple Query Wizard's last step, you enter a query title and determine how to open the query.

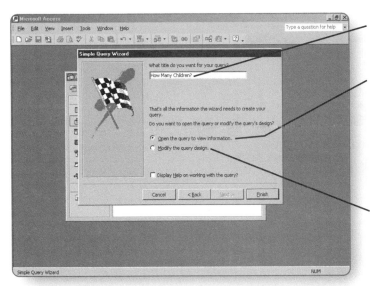

1. **Enter** a **name** for the query in the text box.

2a. **Click** on the **Open the query to view information option button** to open the query in Datasheet view.

OR

2b. **Click** on the **Modify the query design option button** to open the query in Design view.

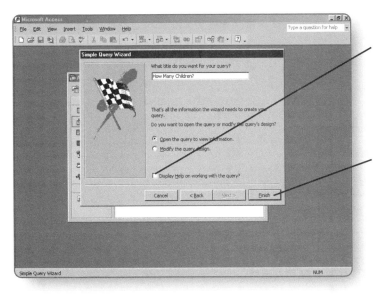

3. (Optional) **Click** on the **Display Help on working with the query check box** to display the help window when you open the query.

4. **Click** on **Finish**. The query will open based on your selection in Step 2.

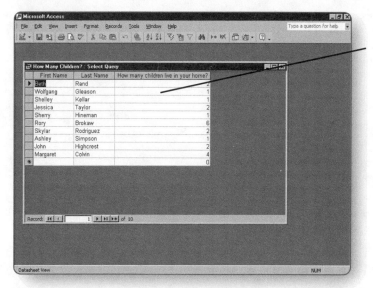

If you choose to open the query in this final wizard step, the query will display the fields you selected in Datasheet view.

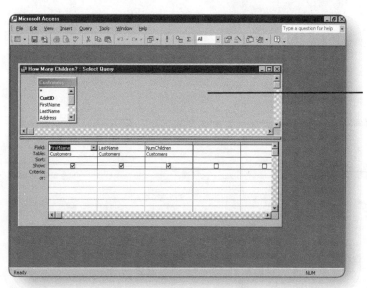

If you choose to modify the query's design in this step, it will open in Design view, in which you can modify and customize the query.

13

Creating a Basic Query in Design View

If you want more flexibility than a query wizard provides, you can create a query from scratch in Design view. In this chapter, you will learn how to:

- Start a query in Design view
- Select a table
- Add fields
- View query results
- Save a query

Starting a Query in Design View

To create a query from scratch, you need to start it in Design view.

1. Click on the **Queries button** in the main database window.

NOTE

If you're new to queries, it's a good idea to draft your query format on paper before creating it in Design view.

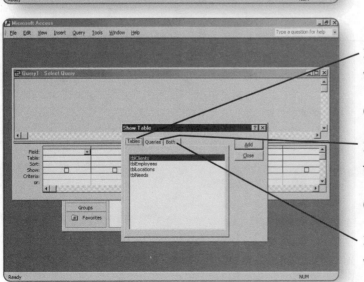

2. Double-click on **Create query in Design view**. The Show Table dialog box will open.

3a. Click on the **Tables tab** to view only tables.

OR

3b. Click on the **Queries tab** to view only queries.

OR

3c. Click on the **Both tab** to view both tables and queries.

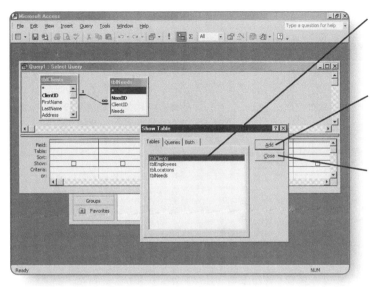

4. Click on the **table or query** you want to include in your new query.

5. Click on **Add**. The table or query will display in the Select Query window.

6. Repeat Steps 4 and **5** until you finish adding the tables and queries.

7. Click on **Close**. The Show Table dialog box will close.

CAUTION

The query will not be meaningful if it contains unrelated tables or queries. If you add multiple tables, make sure that a relationship exists between them. See Chapter 7, "Managing Relationships between Tables."

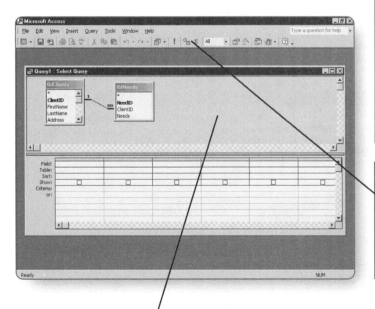

TIP

To reopen the Show Table dialog box, click on the Show Table button on the toolbar.

The top portion of the Select Query window displays each selected table or query. Each selected table or query displays a list of fields that you can add to the query.

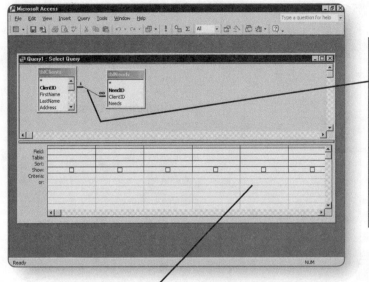

TIP

Relationship lines appear just as they do in the Relationships window. You can create new relationships between tables on the fly by dragging one field to another from the Select Query window.

The bottom portion of the Select Query window displays the design grid. You'll add fields to the query by dragging them from the field lists to the design grid. The design grid is similar to a spreadsheet, with columns representing each field in the query.

Adding Fields

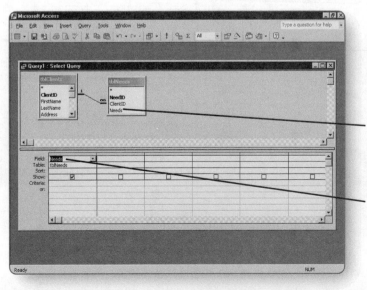

To add fields to your query, you drag them to the design grid. You can include a subset of fields from the displayed tables, or you can include all fields.

1. Click on the **first field** from the field list that you want to include in your query.

2. Drag the **selected field** to a Field row in the design grid. The field will appear in the grid.

TIP

You can also add fields to the grid by double-clicking on them.

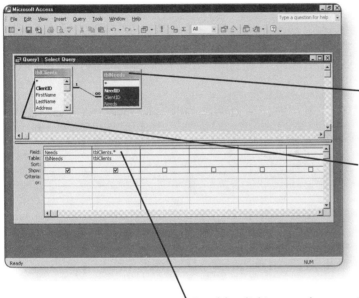

3. Repeat Steps 1 and **2** until you add all desired fields to the design grid.

To select all the fields in the list at once, double-click on the table window's title bar.

To add all fields in a table to the query, double-click on the asterisk at the top of the field list.

Double-clicking on the asterisk places a single entry in the grid that stands for the entire table (all fields).

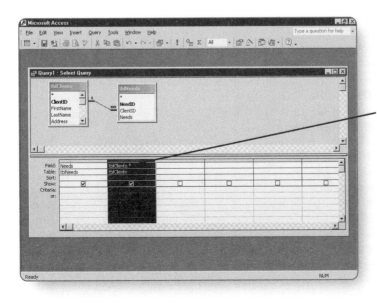

Deleting Fields

You can delete a field from the design grid.

1. Click on the **field selector** for the field. The entire column will be highlighted.

2. Press the **Delete key.** The field will be removed from the grid.

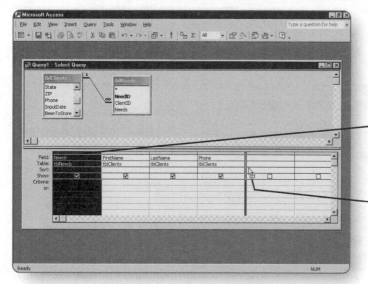

Moving Fields

You can rearrange the order in which the fields appear on the query.

1. Click on the **field selector** for the field. The entire column will be highlighted.

2. Drag the **field** to the left or right, to a new position. The field will appear in the new position.

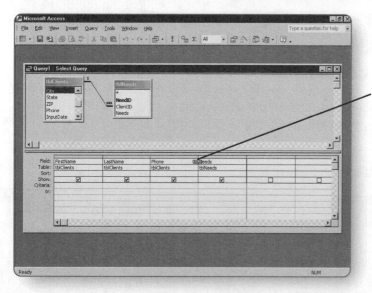

Inserting Fields

To insert a field between two existing fields in the design grid, drag the new field to the column location where you want to insert it.

Viewing Query Results

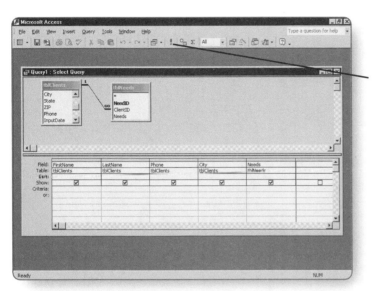

1. Click on the **Run button.**
The query results will appear in
a Datasheet window.

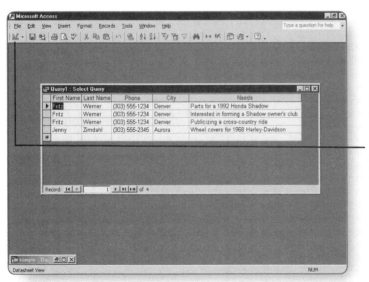

If the results aren't as you
intended, return to Design view
to make further modifications.

2. Click on the **Design View
button.** You will return to Query
Design view.

Saving a Query

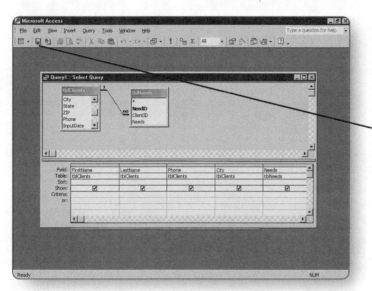

Once you finish your query and verify that the results are what you want, you can save it.

1. **Click** on the **Save button**. The Save As dialog box will open.

2. **Enter** a **name for the query** in the Query Name text box.

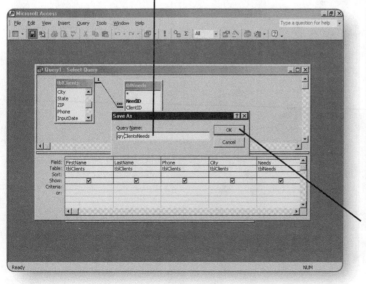

TIP

Although it is not mandatory, most database designers find it advantageous to name all queries starting with "qry" to help distinguish them from tables in object listings.

3. **Click** on **OK**. The query will be saved.

14

Creating Queries That Sort, Filter, or Calculate

Now that you are familiar with Query Design view, you can expand your skills to include queries that not only present selected fields, but also present them in a certain way. You can use queries to sort data, display only certain records based on filter criteria, and perform calculations on field data. In this chapter, you will learn how to:

- Filter query data based on criteria
- Sort query results
- Create a calculated field

Reopening a Query for Editing

To edit a query design that you have already saved and closed, select the query from the Database window and then open it in Design view, the same as you would with a table.

1. **Click** on the **Queries button** in the main database window.

2. **Click** on the **query** you want to edit. The query name will be highlighted.

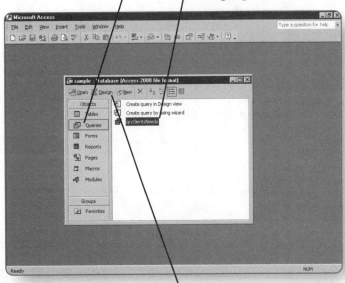

3. **Click** on the **Design button.** The query will open in Query Design view.

Specifying Criteria

You can narrow your query to include only data that matches specific criteria. You might want to display only records with certain field values, for example. You can also use wildcard patterns in your criteria or indicate certain values or ranges to exclude.

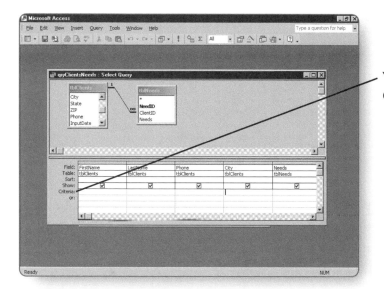

You specify query criteria in the Criteria row in the design grid.

Specifying Exact Matches

To specify an exact match, enter an exact value in the Criteria row of the field column in which you want to search.

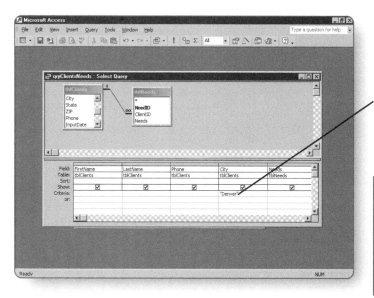

NOTE

You do not have to type the quotation marks; Access will add them automatically.

Specifying Wildcard Patterns

Wildcards offer a way of setting criteria based on patterns or partial words rather than exact matches.

The most common wildcard operators include:

? Replaces a single character.
* Replaces a number of characters.
# Replaces a single digit.

For example, the criterion A* in a FirstName field would include any first name beginning with the letter A, such as Anne, Al, or Adam. The criterion A? would include only the name Al, not Anne nor Adam.

To specify a wildcard pattern, enter the pattern in the Criteria row of the field column in which you want to search.

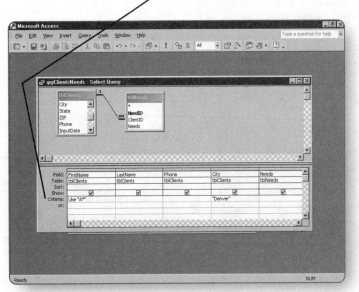

NOTE

You do not have to type *Like* or the quotation marks. Here, only A* was typed, and Access added the rest automatically.

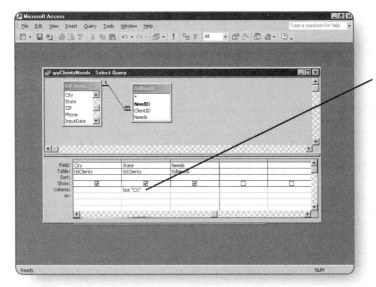

Specifying Eliminations

To specify exclusion criteria, enter **Not** followed by the **elimination term**, for example Not CO. Access automatically adds quotation marks around the phrase.

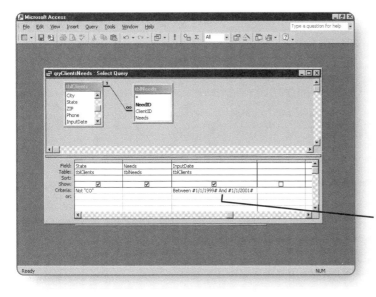

Specifying a Range of Values

To specify more exact dates, you can use the Between...And operator. For example, Between 01/01/99 and 01/01/01 would find all entries including and between these two dates.

You do not have to enter the # signs around the dates; Access does this automatically.

Using OR Criteria

When you enter multiple criteria, all of the criteria must be met in order for a record to be included in the query. If you want to set up multiple criteria and have records included that meet any criterion, use the or line in the query grid.

1. Enter the **first criterion**. It will appear in the Criteria line of the grid.

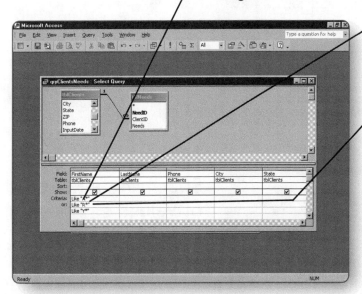

2. Click in the **or line** of the grid, in the column for the field for which you want an "or" criterion.

3. Enter the **additional criterion** in the cell.

4. Repeat Steps 2 and **3** as needed to enter other "or" criteria.

Sorting Query Fields

By default, query fields are not sorted. You can, however, sort any fields in either ascending or descending order.

1. Click on the **Sort row** in the field column you want to sort. A down arrow will appear to the right of the field.

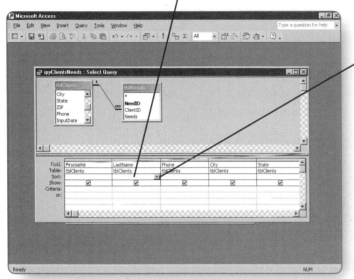

2. Click on the **down arrow**. A menu will appear.

3a. Click on **Ascending** to sort in ascending order.

OR

3b. Click on **Descending** to sort in descending order.

OR

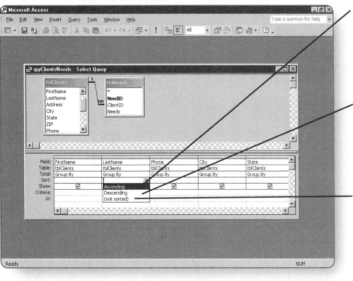

3c. Click on **(not sorted)** to not sort the field.

The sort order will be set based on the instructions in Step 3.

Specifying Calculations

Using a query is a convenient way to perform a calculation on a group of records. For example, you might want to know how many orders each salesperson placed last month or the total dollar amount for these orders. You'll use the Total row in the design grid to specify calculation criteria. (This row does not appear by default; you turn it on by clicking on the Totals button on the toolbar.)

You can specify the following calculation types:

- **Group By**. The default setting for each field; it essentially means "no calculation."

- **Sum**. Totals the values.

- **Avg**. Averages the values.

- **Min**. Finds the minimum value.

- **Max**. Finds the maximum value.

- **Count**. Counts the number of values.

- **StDev**. Calculates the standard deviation of the values.

- **Var**. Calculates the variance of the values.

- **First**. Finds the first field value.

- **Last**. Finds the last field value.

- **Expression**. Creates a calculated field through an expression.

- **Where**. Indicates criteria for a field not included in the query.

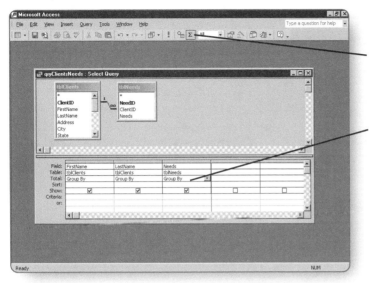

1. **Click** on the **Totals button** on the toolbar. The Total row will appear in the design grid.

2. **Click** on the **Total row** for the first field whose calculation type you want to specify.

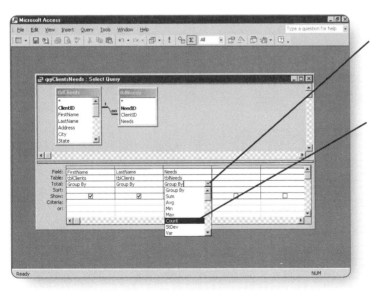

3. **Click** on the **down arrow** to the right of the field. A menu will appear.

4. **Click** on the **calculation type** you want to apply to that field.

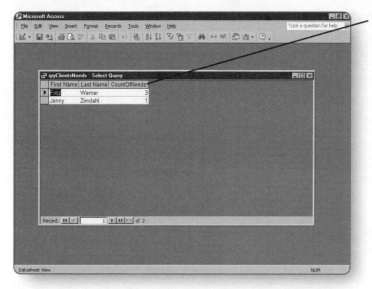

Applying a calculation to a field removes that field's detail from the query. For example, if you specify the Count calculation for the Needs field, instead of each individual need appearing next to each customer's name, a new column containing the number of needs for that customer will appear in the query results.

Part IV Review Questions

1. What are the two sort orders, and how does each one sort? *See "Sorting Data" in Chapter 11*

2. How can you filter your table data based on more than one criterion? *See "Filtering Data" in Chapter 11*

3. How can you quickly find a specific word in a table that contains thousands of records? *See "Finding Data" in Chapter 11*

4. What options does a summary query offer? *See "Choosing a Detail or Summary Query" in Chapter 12*

5. What information appears in the top part of the Query Design window? *See "Starting a Query in Design View" in Chapter 13*

6. How do you delete a field from a query? *See "Deleting Fields" in Chapter 13*

7. In which row of the query design grid do you enter criteria? *See "Specifying Criteria" in Chapter 14*

8. If you want to enter two criteria and include all records that match either one, where do you enter the second criterion? *See "Using OR Criteria" in Chapter 14*

9. What button do you click on to make the Total line display in the query design grid? *See "Specifying Calculations" in Chapter 14*

10. What calculation does the Group By entry in the Total line perform? *See "Specifying Calculations" in Chapter 14*

P A R T   V

Creating and Using Forms

15

Creating an AutoForm

The simplest and easiest way to create a form is to use the AutoForm feature. Using AutoForm, you can automatically create columnar, tabular, and datasheet forms based on a table or query you select. In this chapter, you'll learn how to:

- Choose an AutoForm type
- Create an AutoForm
- Save an AutoForm
- Save and close an AutoForm

Choosing an AutoForm Type

An AutoForm creates a simple form based on the table you specify. You do not have a choice of formatting with an AutoForm, but you can adjust the formatting later in Form Design view if desired. (You will learn about Form Design view in the next chapter.)

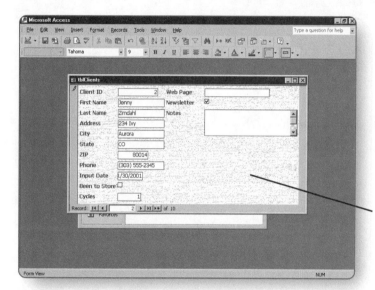

You can create five kinds of AutoForms: Columnar, Tabular, Datasheet, PivotTable, and PivotChart. The latter two are rather specialized, and beginners will seldom use them, so this book does not cover them. The most common types are the first three.

A Columnar form is the most common form type. It presents the fields in one or more columns, with one record displayed at a time.

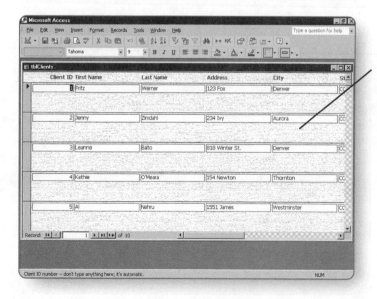

A Tabular form uses boxes for each field, as in a Columnar form, but it presents multiple records at a time in a row-and-column format.

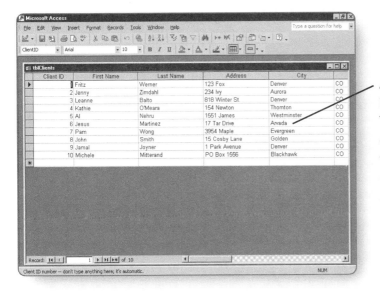

A Datasheet form is virtually identical to a regular datasheet. You might use it if you like to enter data using a datasheet but want the fields (columns) in a different order or if you want a subset of the fields displayed.

Creating an AutoForm

The procedure for creating each of the types of AutoForms is very similar. You use the New Form dialog box in each case.

1. Click on the **Forms button** in the main database window.

2. Click on **New**. The New Form dialog box will open.

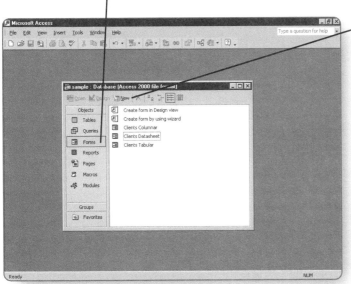

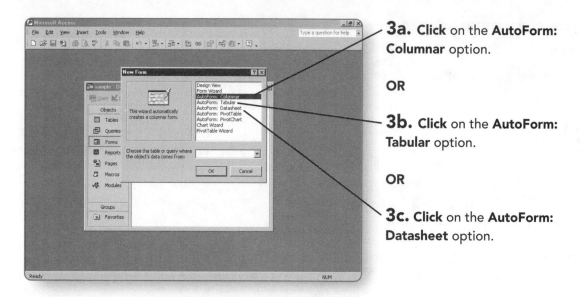

3a. Click on the **AutoForm: Columnar** option.

OR

3b. Click on the **AutoForm: Tabular** option.

OR

3c. Click on the **AutoForm: Datasheet** option.

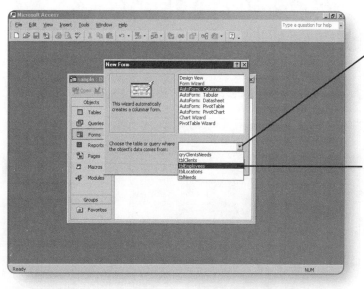

4. Click on the **down arrow** next to the Choose the table or query where the object's data comes from list box. A menu will appear.

5. Click on the **desired table**.

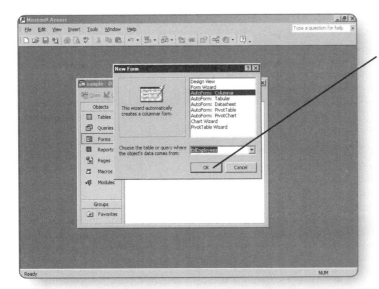

6. Click on **OK**.

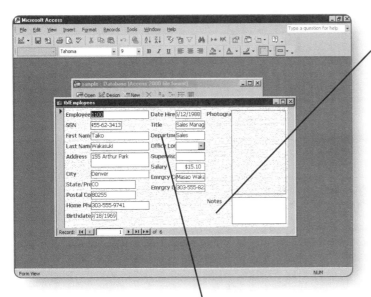

A columnar form based on this table will appear in Form view. You can begin entering data in the form immediately if you want. Or you can modify its appearance to suit your needs.

NOTE

Don't worry if field names and field entries appear truncated. You can modify the form layout later.

Saving a Form

Once you create a form, you'll want to save it.

1. Click on the **Save button**. The Save As dialog box will open.

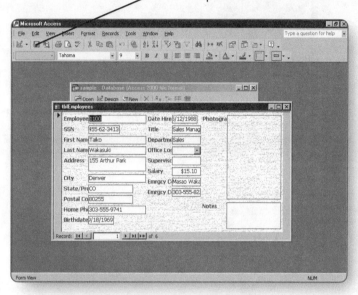

2. Enter a **name** for your form in the Form Name text box.

3. Click on **OK**. The form will be saved, but will remain open.

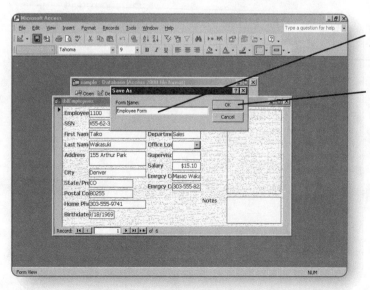

Saving and Closing a Form

You can also save and close a form at the same time.

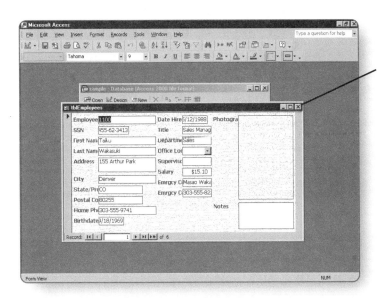

1. **Click** on the **Close button** on the form. A warning dialog box will appear.

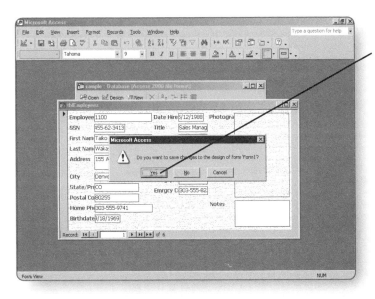

2. **Click** on **Yes** to save the form. The Save As dialog box will open.

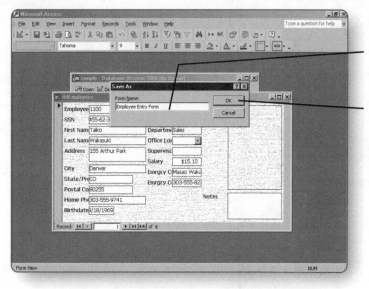

3. Enter a **name** for your form in the Form Name text box.

4. Click on **OK**. The form will be saved and closed simultaneously.

16

Entering Data in a Form

Now that you have created a basic form, you need to learn how to enter data into it. In this chapter, you'll learn how to:

- Open a form in Form view
- Navigate among fields in a form
- Enter data into a form

Opening a Form in Form View

To enter data in a form, you need to open the form in Form view.

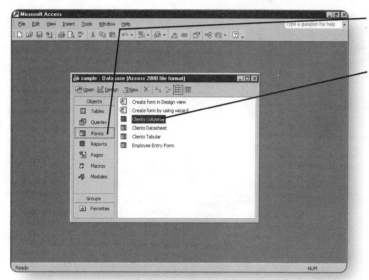

1. **Click** on the **Forms button** in the main database window.

2. **Double-click** on the **form** that you want to open. It will open in Form view.

Navigating in Form View

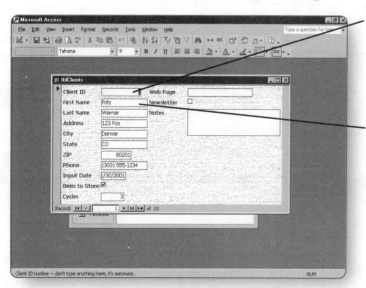

When you open a form, the first record in the associated table appears, with the first field in the record selected.

To move to another field, click in the field you want or press the Tab key to move to the next field. To move back to the previous field, press Shift+Tab.

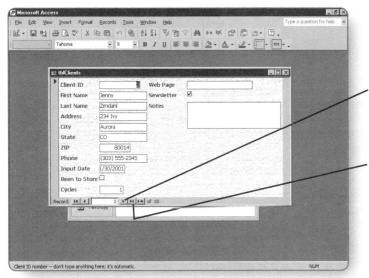

To move to the next record, click on the Next Record button at the bottom of the window.

To move quickly ahead to the last record, click on the Last Record button.

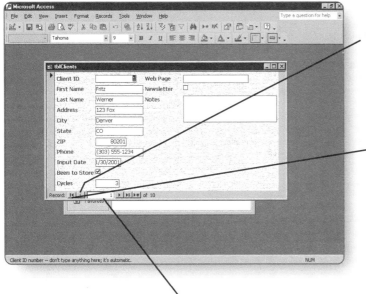

To move back to the previous record, click on the Previous Record button.

To move to the first record again, click on the First Record button.

You can also type a specific record number in the Record number box to move to that record.

Entering a New Record in a Form

To start a new record, display a blank form and then type the data into the field boxes provided.

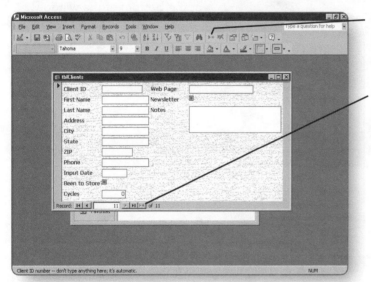

1. Click on the **New Record button**. A blank form record will appear.

You can also use the **New Record** button at the bottom of the window.

2. Enter data in the new form.

TIP

Access automatically enters the next consecutive number in an Auto-Number field.

---

3. Repeat Steps 1 and **2** until you finish adding records.

17

Creating a Form with the Form Wizard

The Form Wizard helps you build a basic form while offering step-by-step guidance. Using this wizard, you can quickly create a basic form by specifying the fields you want to include, as well as the form layout and style. In this chapter, you'll learn how to:

- Start the Form Wizard
- Select fields for your form
- Choose a form layout
- Choose a form style
- Finish the form

Starting the Form Wizard

The Form Wizard can help you select the fields, layout, and style for your form.

1. Click on the **Forms button** in the main database window.

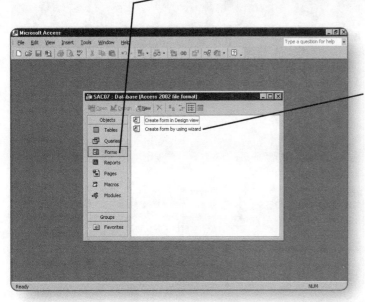

2. Double-click on **Create form by using wizard** within the window. The Form Wizard will open.

Selecting Fields for Your Form

After you open the wizard, you select specific fields to place in your form. Using the Form Wizard, you can select fields from more than one table or query.

TIP

Before creating a form, think carefully about the fields you need to include. Including all the fields in a specific table or query will often overcrowd a form, or the fields may not all fit.

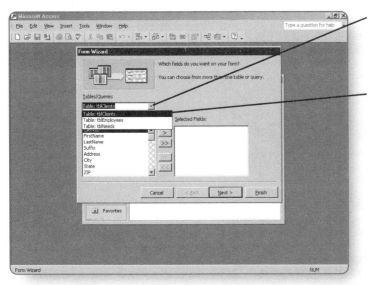

1. **Click** on the **down arrow** to the right of the Tables/Queries list box. A menu will appear.

2. **Click** on the **table or query** from which you want to select a field. A list of the fields for that table/query will appear.

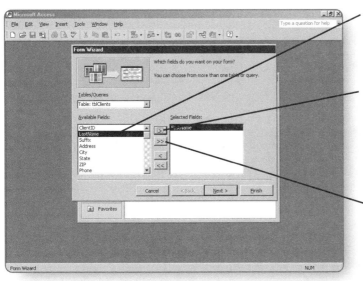

3. **Click** on a **field** that you want to include on the form. The field will be highlighted.

4. **Click** on the **right arrow button**. The field will move to the Selected Fields list.

TIP

Click on the double right arrow button to include all available fields in your form.

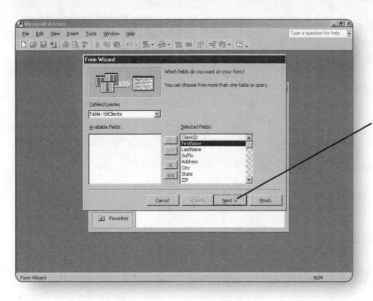

5. Repeat Steps 1 through **4** until you've selected all the fields you want to include in your form.

6. Click on **Next**. The Form Wizard will continue to the next step.

Choosing a Form Layout

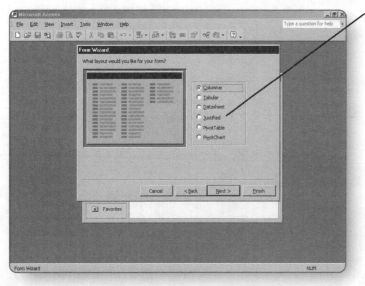

You can choose from six different form layouts:

- **Columnar**. Each field displays on its own line preceded by a label.

- **Tabular**. For each record, the fields display on one line with labels on the top row.

- **Datasheet**. The fields display as a table datasheet using rows and columns.

- **Justified**. The fields for each record display justified in the form.

- **PivotTable**. A PivotTable grid appears in which you can drop fields. This form type is beyond the scope of this book.

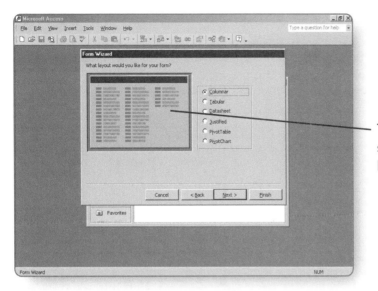

- **PivotChart**. A PivotChart grid appears in which you can drop fields. This form type is also beyond the scope of this book.

The preview box displays a sample of what the selected layout will look like.

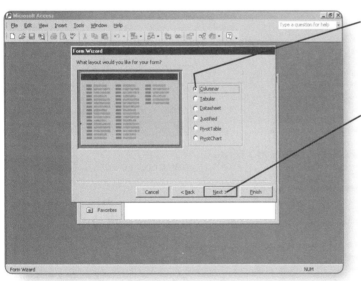

1. Click on the **form layout option button** for the format that you want to apply to your form.

2. Click on **Next** to continue.

Choosing a Form Style

Access includes several predefined form styles from which you can choose. The 10 form styles range from casual to serious and include both colors and gray tones.

TIP

Be sure that the form style you choose is consistent with existing forms and reports in your database. Style consistency will make your database easier to use and more pleasing to look at.

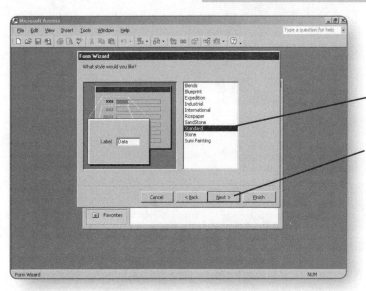

1. Click on the **form style** you want to display on your form.

2. Click on **Next** to continue.

Finishing the Form

In the final step of the Form Wizard, you enter a form title and determine how to display your finished form.

1. Enter the **title** you want to display on your form in the text box.

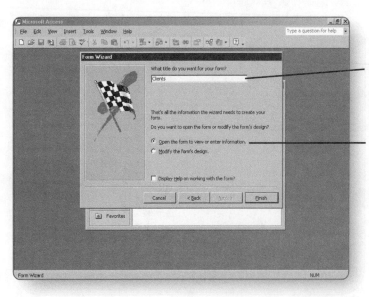

2a. Click on the **Open the form to view or enter information option button**. The form will open in Form view.

OR

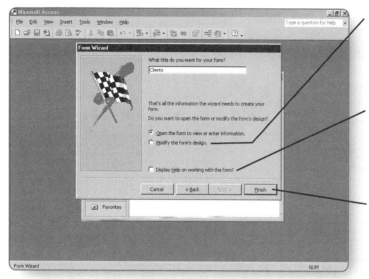

2b. Click on the **Modify the form's design option button**. The form will open in Design view.

3. Click on the **Display Help on working with the form check box** if you want to automatically open a help window.

4. Click on **Finish**. Depending on the option you selected in Step 2, Access will display the form in either Form view or Design view.

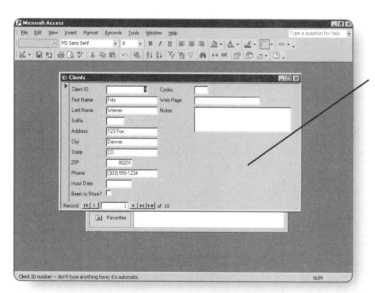

This is an example of Form view, which you learned about in Chapter 16, "Entering Data in a Form."

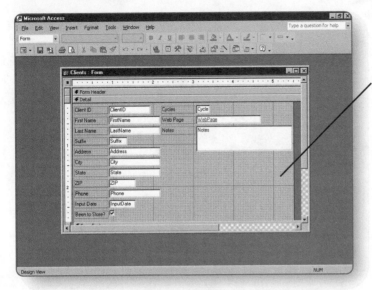

Here is an example of Design view, which you will learn about in Chapter 18, "Changing a Form's Appearance."

18

Changing a Form's Appearance

After you create a form with the Form Wizard or AutoForm feature, you can change its default style or customize its formatting. In this chapter, you will learn how to:

- Open a form in Design view
- Change a form's format
- Add text boxes
- Modify fonts
- Bold, italicize, and underline
- Set alignment

Opening a Form in Design View

To modify the design of an existing form, open it in Design view. In this view, you can apply a special format; modify fonts; bold, italicize, or underline text; set alignment; and more.

1. Click on the **Forms button** in the main database window.

2. Click on the **form you want to modify**. It will be highlighted.

3. Click on the **Design button**. The form will open in Design view.

NOTE

You can also open a form in Design view in the final step of the Form Wizard, as you saw at the end of the preceding chapter.

You will notice in Design view that a form consists of controls placed in specific sections.

A Form Header displays information, such as labels, at the top of a form. The Form Wizard does not place anything here by default.

Every form includes a Detail section, which presents the records.

A Form Footer area enables you to enter labels or other information that should appear at the bottom of the form. The Form Footer remains onscreen at all times, even if you scroll down on a long form.

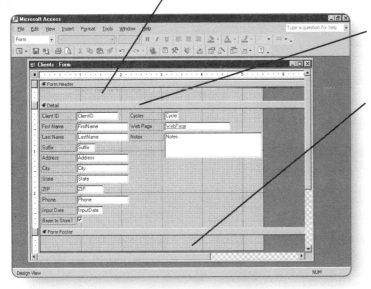

A *label* is a descriptive bit of text. This one, for example, shows the name of the field to its right.

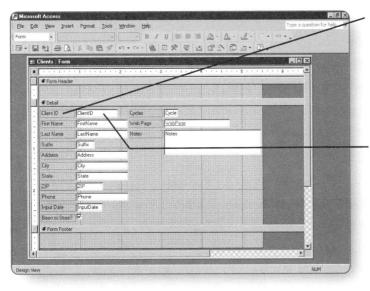

A *text box* also contains text, but it is associated with something "behind the scenes," such as a field in a table. Labels and text boxes commonly work in pairs, but can also appear separately from one another.

> **NOTE**
> There are other types of form controls, such as option buttons, list boxes, and combo boxes. You will learn about them in the next several chapters.

Displaying the Toolbox

The Toolbox is a floating toolbar containing buttons for various types of controls you can insert. If it does not appear, you must display it before you can add anything to your form.

1. **Click** on the **Toolbox button** on the toolbar.

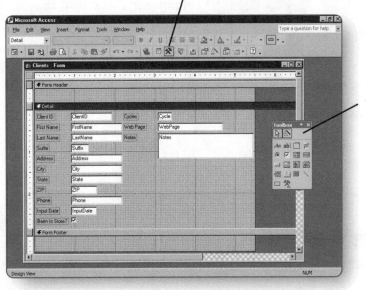

The Toolbox will appear.

Adding a Label

In addition to the labels for each field, you might want to place additional labels on your form. A prime example would be to place a form title in the Form Header area.

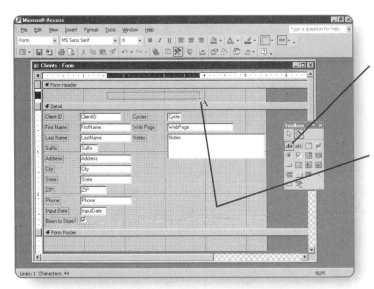

1. Click on the **Label button** in the Toolbox. The mouse pointer will turn into a crosshair with a capital A attached.

2. Drag on the **form** where you want the text box to appear. The label box will appear on the form.

3. Type text in the box.

TIP

Don't worry if the text is the wrong size or color or the background of the box isn't what you want. You will learn to format text on a form in the section "Changing Text Properties," later in this chapter.

Changing a Form's Format

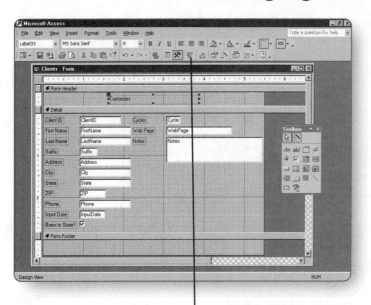

The Form Wizard and AutoForm features help you choose a style to apply to your form. The style you choose in the Form Wizard is actually an AutoFormat. An *AutoFormat* uses predefined colors, borders, fonts, and font sizes designed to look good together and convey a specific image. You can always change the AutoFormatting if you don't like the default styles or the style you originally chose.

1. Click on the **AutoFormat button**. The AutoFormat dialog box will open with the current format highlighted.

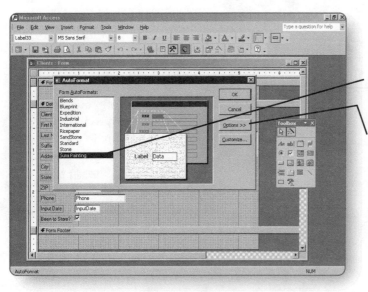

2. Click on a **new form format** in the Form AutoFormats list.

3. Click on the **Options button** in the AutoFormat dialog box. The dialog box will extend to include the Attributes to Apply group box. By default, all attributes are selected.

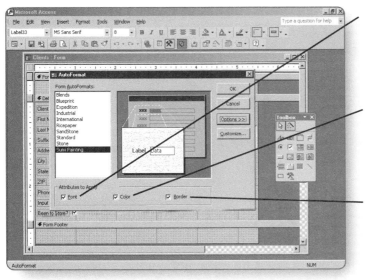

4. **Click** on the **Font check box** if you want to remove the check mark and prevent formatting changes to fonts.

5. **Click** on the **Color check box** if you want to remove the check mark and prevent color-formatting changes.

6. **Click** on the **Border check box** if you want to remove the check mark and prevent border-formatting changes.

7. **Click** on **OK** to accept your formatting changes.

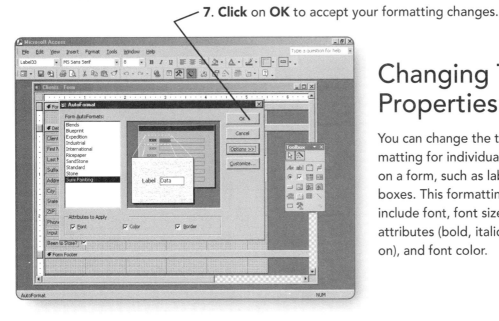

Changing Text Properties

You can change the text formatting for individual controls on a form, such as labels or text boxes. This formatting can include font, font size, font attributes (bold, italic, and so on), and font color.

Changing the Font

The Font drop-down list on the Formatting toolbar controls your form's fonts.

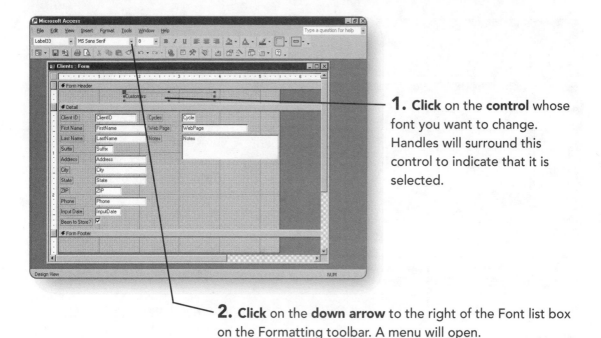

1. Click on the **control** whose font you want to change. Handles will surround this control to indicate that it is selected.

2. Click on the **down arrow** to the right of the Font list box on the Formatting toolbar. A menu will open.

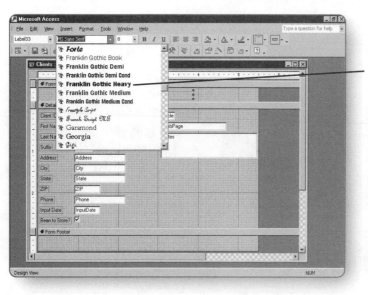

3. Click on a **new font.**

The control text will appear in the new font.

Changing the Font Size

The Font Size drop-down list on the Formatting toolbar controls font size.

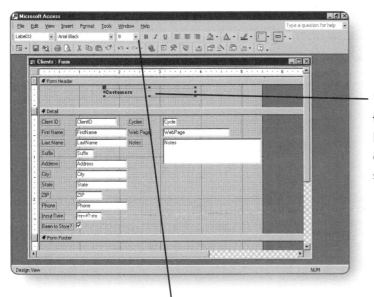

1. Click on the **control** whose font size you want to change. Handles will surround this control to indicate that it is selected.

2. Click on the **down arrow** to the right of the Font Size list box. A menu will appear.

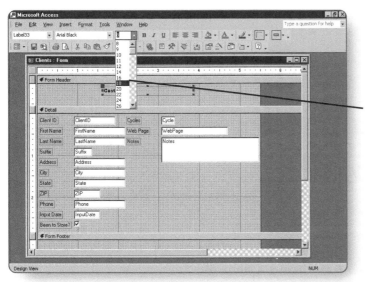

3. Click on a **new font size**.

The control text will appear in the new font size.

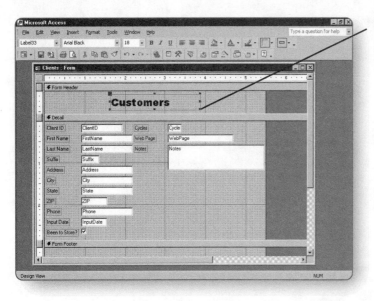

4. Drag a **handle** (a black square) to enlarge the control's frame if needed.

Changing the Font Color

The Font/Fore Color button on the Formatting toolbar controls font color.

1. Click on the **control whose font color** you want to modify. Handles will surround this control to indicate that it is selected.

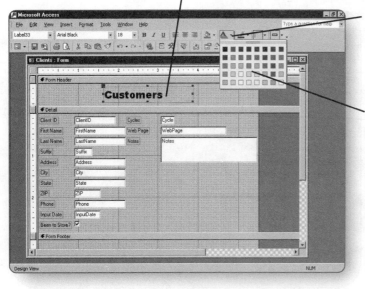

2. Click on the **down arrow** to the right of the Font/Fore Color button. The font color palette will open.

3. Click on the **color you want to apply** from the font color palette. The control text will appear in the new font color.

Changing Text Attributes

You can also modify the appearance of a form by bolding, italicizing, and underlining controls that contain text.

1. **Click** on the **control** you want to bold. It will be selected.

2a. **Click** on the **Bold** button.

OR

2b. **Click** on the **Italic** button.

OR

2c. **Click** on the **Underline** button.

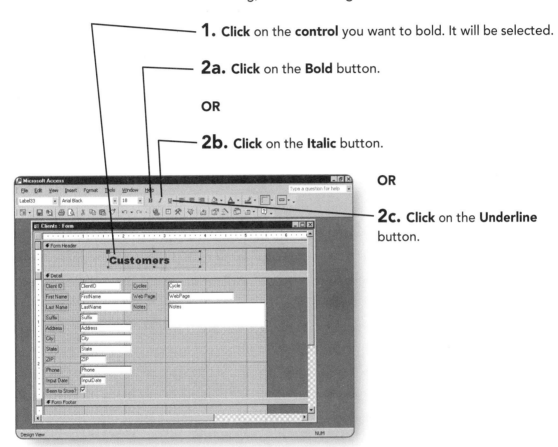

Setting Alignment

On Access forms, you can align controls to the left, center, or right.

1. Click on the **control** whose alignment you want to set.

2a. Click on the **Align Left button** to left-align the text.

OR

2b. Click on the **Align Center button** to center the selected text.

OR

2c. Click on the **Align Right button** to right-align the text. The control will be aligned.

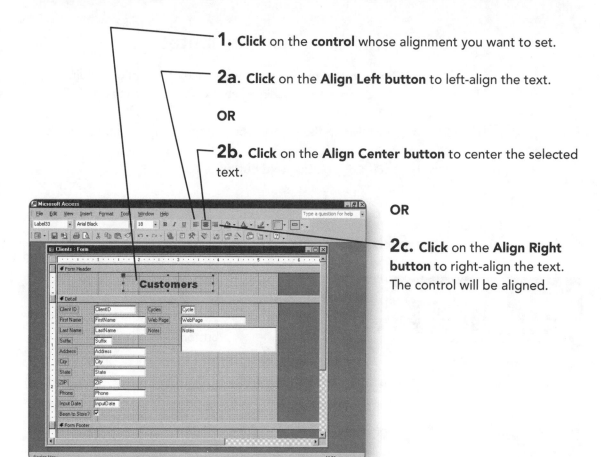

Setting Background Color

You can set a background color for a section of the form (Form Header, Detail, or Form Footer) or for an individual control. Simply select what you want and then apply a color to it.

Selecting a Form Section

Before you can apply a background to a section of the form, you must select it.

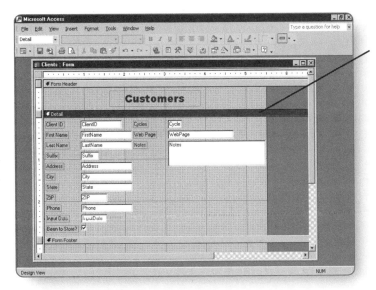

To select a particular section, click on its name. The bar will be highlighted.

Applying a Background Color

A background color applies to the selected section(s) or to an individual control if a control is selected when you issue the command.

1. Select the **control** or **section** to which you want the background to apply.

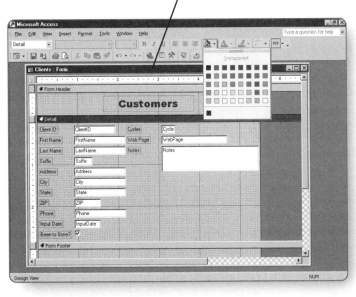

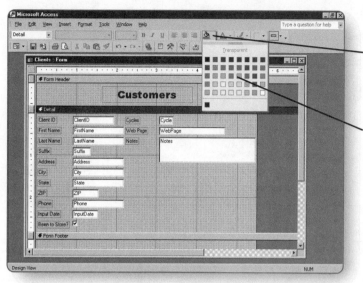

2. Click on the **down arrow** on the Fill/Back Color button. A palette of colors will open.

3. Click on the **color** you want to apply. The color will be applied to the selected section or control.

TIP

You can click on the View button to go to Form view to preview your changes. Click on the same button again to return to Design view.

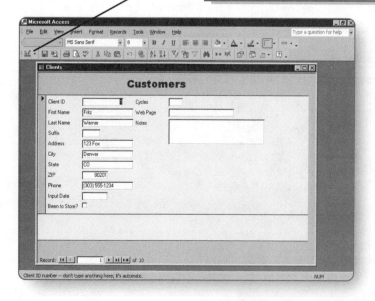

19

Working with Form Fields

In Design view, you can further customize your form by adding fields and other controls. This chapter will work with fields; Chapter 20, "Adding Special Control Types," will cover other control types. The skills you learn in this chapter will apply to the different control types in Chapter 20 as well. In this chapter, you will learn how to:

- Add fields to forms
- Reposition fields
- Resize fields and field labels
- Delete fields from a form

Adding and Removing Fields

To add or remove fields on a form, you start in Form Design view; refer to Chapter 18, "Changing a Form's Appearance," if you need help opening a form in Design view.

Displaying the Field List

The field list might appear automatically in Form Design view. If it does not, you can display it.

1. Click on the **Field List button** on the toolbar.

> **TIP**
>
> If you need to add or remove more than one or two additional fields or controls, it's usually easier to create a new form using the Form Wizard because of the difficulty of getting the fields precisely aligned on the form grid.

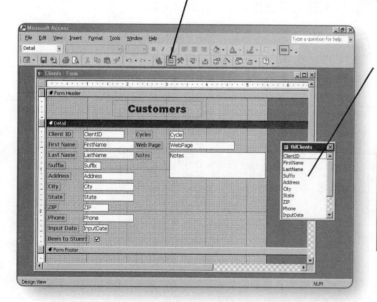

The field list will appear in a floating box.

> **TIP**
>
> You can drag the field list around onscreen by its title bar as desired.

Adding a Field

You might not have added all the available fields to the form when you initially created it. You can add other fields at any time.

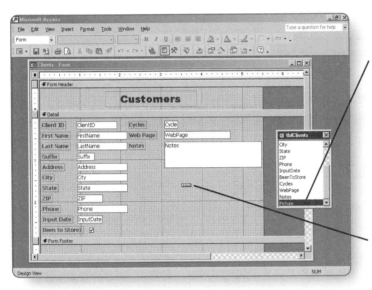

1. Click on the **field** in the field list that you want to include on your form.

2. Drag the **field** to the location on the form where you want to place it.

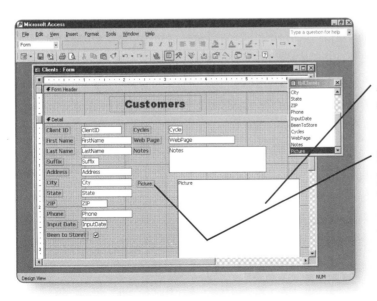

A control for that field will appear on the form.

Depending on the field type, you might want to edit the label text or even delete the label altogether if it's obvious what the field represents. ("Picture" is a good example.)

> **TIP**
> Any formatting you have applied to other labels on the form will not automatically transfer to the new field. You can use the Format Painter button to copy formatting from an existing label to the new one if desired.

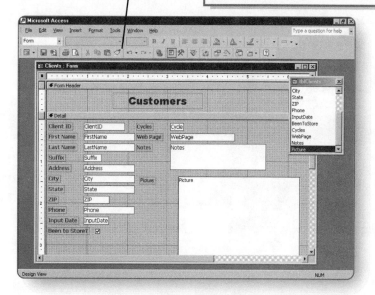

Moving Controls

All controls on a form—including fields—can be easily dragged around, just like graphics in a program such as Microsoft Word or Microsoft PowerPoint. The only tricky part when working with fields specifically is that most fields have two components: the field itself and an associated text label containing the field name. These pieces can be moved either separately or as a pair.

Moving the Field and Label Together

The field and its label are linked so that when you click on one of them to select it, the other one also is selected. You can easily move them as a pair.

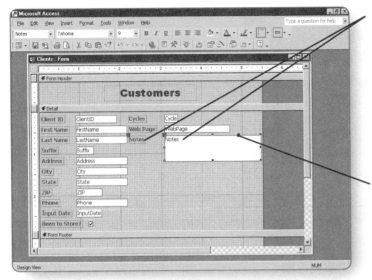

1. Click on the **field** or its **label**. Both will be selected.

The object you clicked on will have a full set of selection handles; the associated object will have only a single selection handle in its upper-left corner.

2. Position the **mouse pointer** over the object you clicked on so that the mouse pointer becomes an open hand.

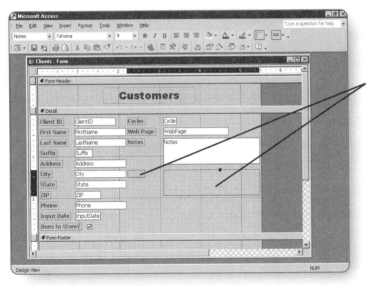

3. Drag the **field and label** to the new location. They will move as a single unit.

Moving the Field or Label Separately

You can move a field only or its label only, without the associated item. For example, you might want to place a field's label above it instead of to its left.

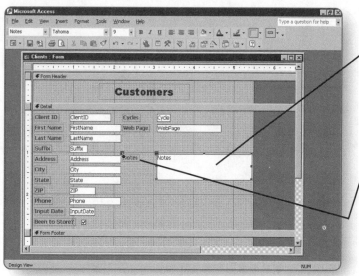

1. Click on the **field** or its **label**. Both will be selected.

2. Position the **mouse pointer** over the upper-left selection handle of the item to move. The mouse pointer will become a pointing hand.

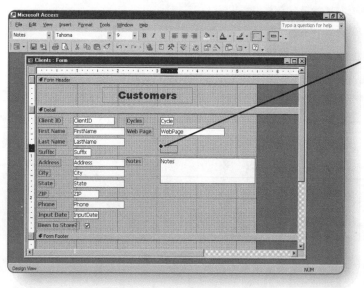

3. Drag the **field** or **label** to the new location. The associated item will not move.

Moving Multiple Controls at Once

You can select several controls together and move them as a group. This helps keep the spacing consistent between controls.

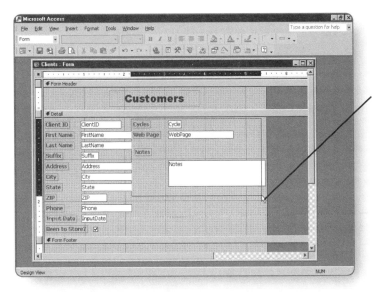

1. **Drag** a **box** around the fields you want to select. All fields that fall within that area will be selected.

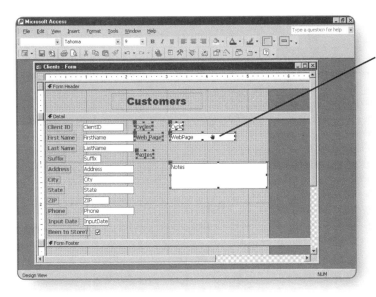

2. **Position** the **mouse pointer** over any selected field. The mouse pointer will become an open hand.

3. **Drag** the **fields** to the new location.

Resizing a Field or Other Control

Resizing a control on a form is just like resizing an object in other Microsoft Office programs such as Word and PowerPoint. Unlike with moving, a field and its associated label do not resize as a pair; you resize each object separately.

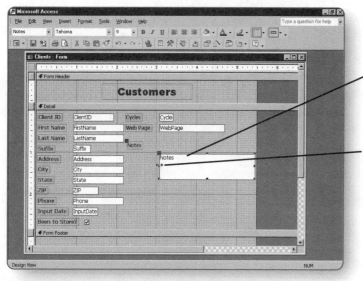

1. Click on the **control** that you want to resize. Selection handles will appear around it.

2. Point to **any selection handle** except the upper-left one. The mouse pointer will become a double-headed arrow.

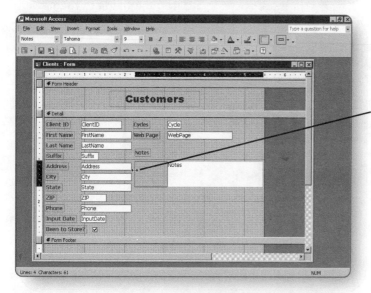

3. Drag the **selection handle** to resize the control.

Deleting a Field or Other Control

You can delete a control on a form. You can delete an entire field, including its label, or you can delete only the label, leaving the field behind. The latter might be useful if a certain field is self-explanatory and does not require a label.

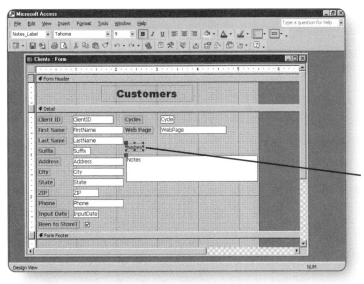

NOTE

You cannot delete the field but leave its associated label; the label automatically goes away when the field does.

1. Click on the **control you want to delete**. Selection handles will appear around it.

2. Press the **Delete key** on your keyboard. The object will disappear.

20

Adding Special Control Types

You can use option groups, combo boxes, and list boxes on a form to make it easier for users to select and enter data. In this chapter, you will learn how to:

- Add option groups to forms
- Understand combo boxes and list boxes
- Create a combo box or list box that will look up values
- Create a combo box or list box in which you enter values

Adding Option Groups

One type of control you can add to a form is an option group. An option group lets a user choose one of several displayed options. Option buttons usually precede the options, but you can also use check boxes or toggles. You enter the actual options as label names for the option group.

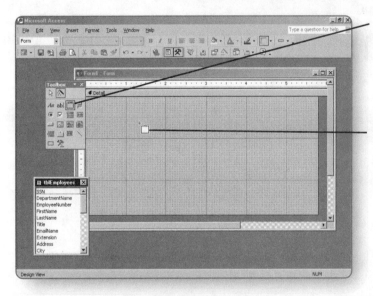

1. Click on the **Option Group button** in the Toolbox to activate it. The mouse pointer will become a crosshair with a box.

2. Click on the **area of the form** where you want to place the box. The Option Group Wizard will open.

TIP

If this is the first time you are adding an option group to a form and you used the default install, Access might prompt you to install this feature. Insert your Office CD into your CD-ROM drive and click on Yes to install.

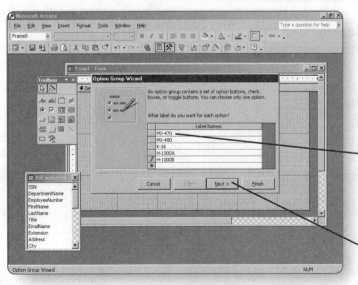

3. Type the **label name** for each option button you want to display in the text box in the Label Names column.

4. Click on **Next** to continue.

Specifying a Default Choice

You can indicate a default option that will display for every record, but it isn't required.

1a. Choose a **field** in the drop-down list next to the Yes, the default choice is option button to indicate the default.

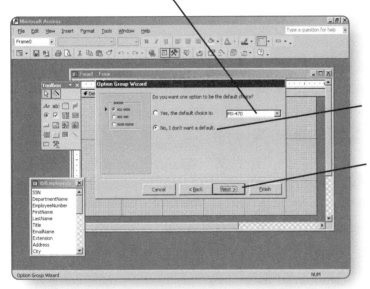

OR

1b. Click on the **No, I don't want a default option button**.

2. Click on **Next** to continue.

Setting Option Values

You assign a numeric value to each option in an option group. Access then saves this numeric value for later use or stores it in a table. The default numeric value series is 1, 2, 3, and so on.

1. Enter the **option value** for each label name in the Values column or leave the defaults.

2. Click on **Next**. The wizard will continue to the next step.

Saving or Storing the Option Group Value

You can either save the option group value for future use or store it in another form field.

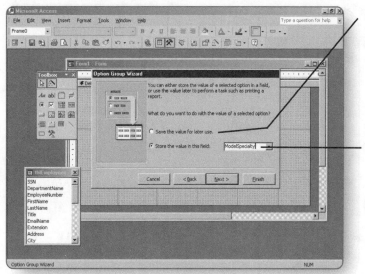

1a. **Click** on the **Save the value for later use option button** to save the value in memory for future use.

OR

1b. **Choose** a **field** in the drop-down list next to the Store the value in this field option button to indicate where to store the value.

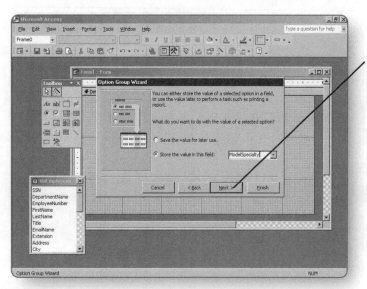

2. **Click** on **Next** to continue.

Specifying Controls and Styles

You can display your options as option buttons, check boxes, or toggle buttons. You can also choose one of five different box styles.

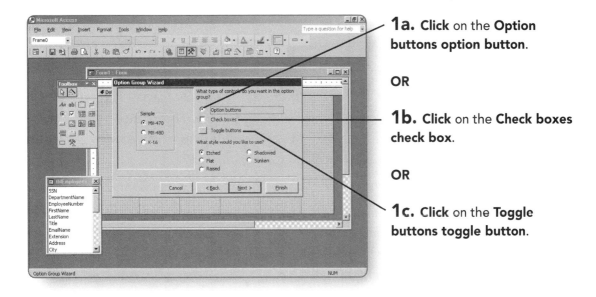

1a. Click on the **Option buttons option button**.

OR

1b. Click on the **Check boxes check box**.

OR

1c. Click on the **Toggle buttons toggle button**.

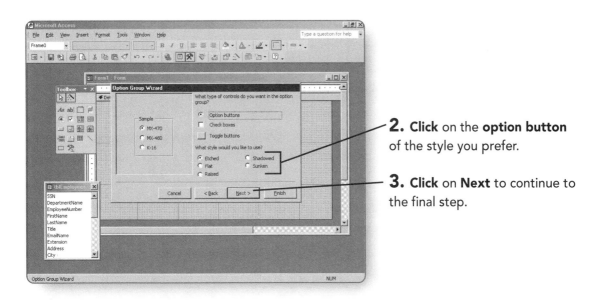

2. Click on the **option button** of the style you prefer.

3. Click on **Next** to continue to the final step.

Finishing the Option Group

In the final step of the Option Group Wizard, you'll create a label for the option group and specify help options.

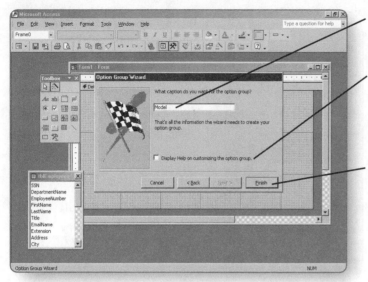

1. **Enter** a **name** for your option group in the text box.

2. **Click** on the **Display Help on customizing the option group check box** if you want to display a help window.

3. **Click** on **Finish**.

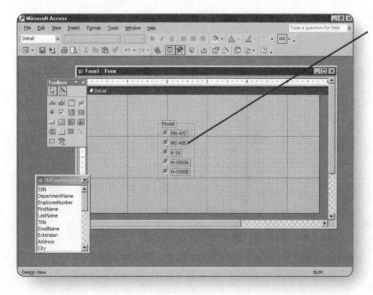

The option group will appear on the form.

Understanding Combo and List Boxes

Combo boxes and list boxes, like option buttons, enable you to provide a range of choices for the user entering records. A list box limits data entry to the choices you provide, while a combo box allows the user to enter new values as well. The process for creating list boxes and combo boxes is nearly identical.

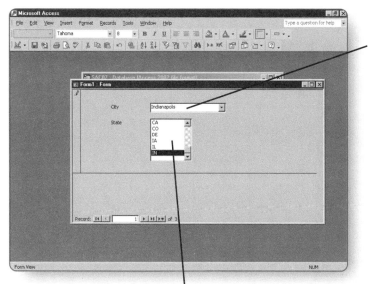

A combo box is a text box with a drop-down list. You can type in the text box or click on its down arrow to open a list from which to choose. For example, you could provide a list of major cities, but allow entry of customers who live in smaller towns as well.

A list box forces you to choose from the preentered values. For example, if your company is authorized to do business only in certain states, you can make sure that no customers are entered who do not live in one of those states.

You can create combo boxes or list boxes that work in different ways. The box can:

- Look up values in a related table or query. For example, on an Orders form, you might want to create a control that lists all the values of the CustomerName field in a Customer table.

- Display a list of values that you enter. In this type of control, you enter whatever values you want, and you aren't limited to what already exists in a table or query.

- Find a record in your form that is based on the value you select in your combo or list box.

This chapter covers the first two of these methods. You can experiment with the third type on your own.

Creating Combo or List Boxes That Look Up Values

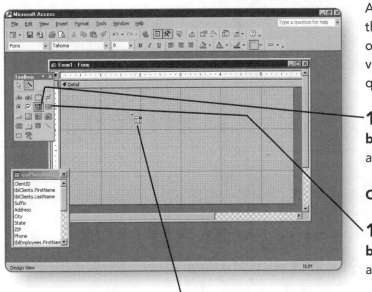

A wizard will guide you through the process of creating combo or list boxes that will look up values in a specified table or query.

1a. Click on the **Combo Box button** in the Toolbox to activate it.

OR

1b. Click on the **List Box button** in the Toolbox to activate it.

2. Click on the **area of the form** where you want to place the box. The Combo Box Wizard or List Box Wizard will open, depending on your selection in Step 1.

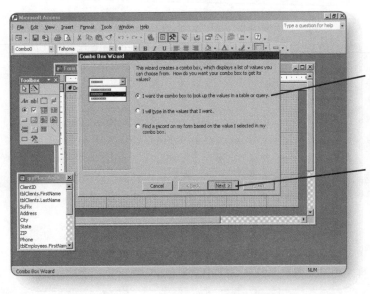

3. Click on the **I want the combo box (or list box) to look up the values in a table or query option button.**

4. Click on **Next** to continue.

Choosing a Table or Query

Next, you'll choose a table or query that contains the combo box or list box values.

1a. **Click** on the **Tables option button** in the View group box to display only tables.

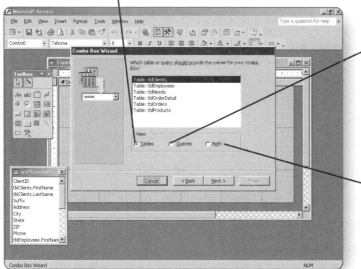

OR

1b. **Click** on the **Queries option button** in the View group box to display only queries.

OR

1c. **Click** on the **Both option button** in the View group box to display both tables and queries.

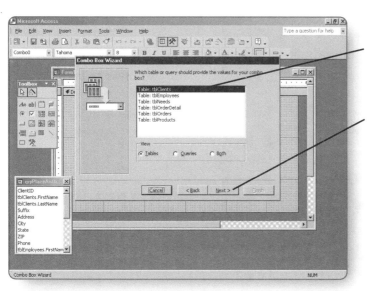

2. **Click** on the **table or query** that contains the values for the combo box or list box.

3. **Click** on **Next** to continue.

Selecting Fields

Next, you'll select the fields to include as combo box or list box columns.

1. Choose the **first field** that you want to include from the Available Fields list.

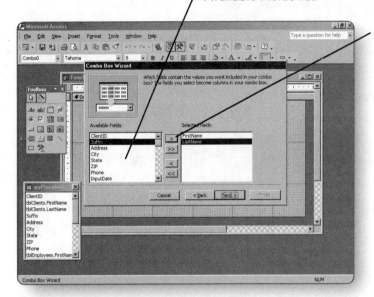

2. Click on the **right arrow button**. The field will move to the Selected Fields list.

3. Repeat Steps 1 and **2** until you select all the fields that you want to include in your combo box or list box.

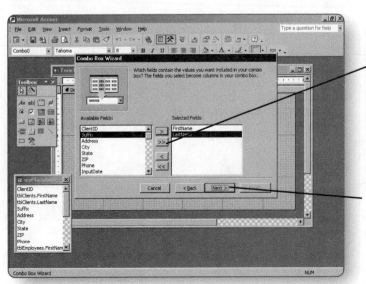

TIP

Click on the double right arrow button to include all available fields in your combo box or list box.

4. Click on **Next**. The wizard will continue to the next step.

Specifying Column Width

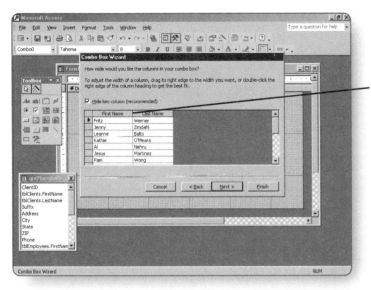

Now, you'll specify how wide to make the columns in your combo box or list box.

1. **Place** the **mouse pointer** on the right edge of an existing column.

2. **Drag** the **column** to the appropriate width.

> ### TIP
> Double-click on the column's right edge to get the best fit.

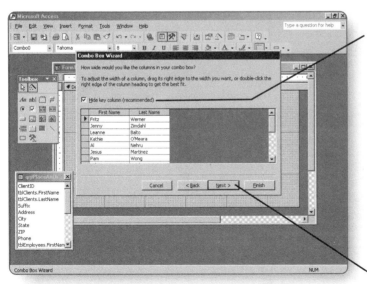

3. **Leave** the **Hide key column (recommended) check box selected** to hide the primary key column.

> ### NOTE
> You'll usually want to hide the primary key column because it doesn't contain actual data.

4. **Click** on **Next** to continue.

Determining What to Do with the Value

You can either save the combo box or list box value for future use or store it in another field.

1a. **Click** on the **Remember the value for later use option button** to save the value in memory for future use.

NOTE

Beginners will probably not use this option because it requires additional work to use the stored value.

OR

1b. **Click** on the **Store that value in this field option button** and then click on the down arrow to the right of the text box. A menu will appear.

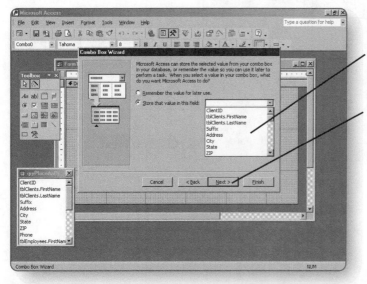

OR

1c. **Click** on a **field** in which to store the value.

2. **Click** on **Next** to continue.

Finishing the Combo Box or List Box

In the final wizard step, you'll create a label for the combo box or list box.

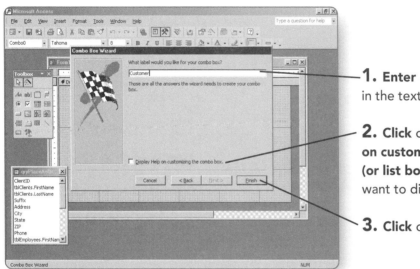

1. **Enter** a **name** for your box in the text box.

2. **Click** on the **Display Help on customizing the combo box (or list box) check box** if you want to display a help window.

3. **Click** on **Finish**.

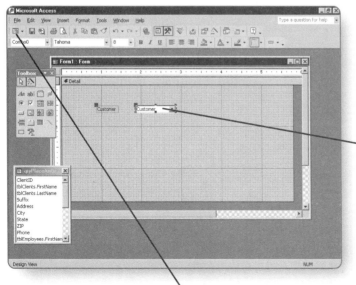

The box will appear on the form.

To try out the new control, click on the View button to switch to Form view.

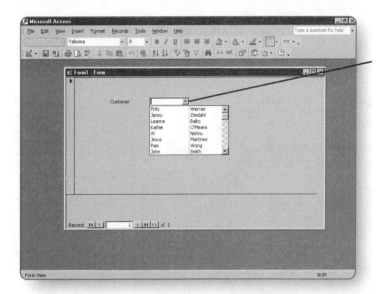

In Form view, click on the down arrow to open the list.

Creating a Combo Box or List Box in Which You Enter Values

You can also create a combo box or list box in which you can enter the box values directly rather than take them from an existing report or query. For example, you might want to have users select from a list that displays the past three years, your company's branch locations, or the products you make.

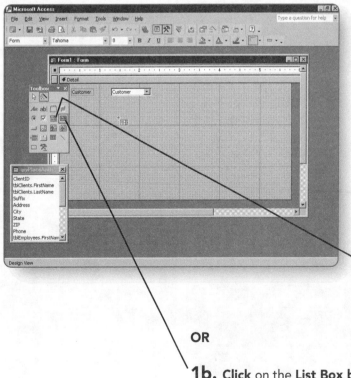

1a. **Click** on the **Combo Box** button in the Toolbox to activate it.

OR

1b. **Click** on the **List Box button** in the Toolbox to activate it.

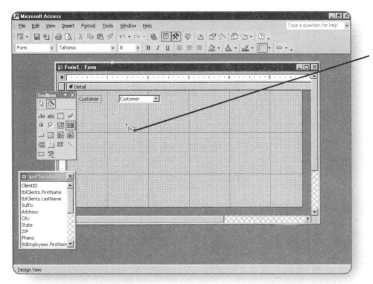

2. Click on the **area of the form** where you want to place the box. The wizard will open.

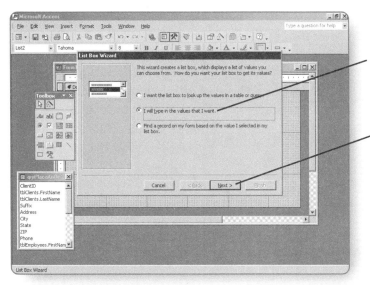

3. Click on the **I will type in the values that I want option button**.

4. Click on **Next** to continue.

Entering the Box Values

Next, you'll enter the values that you want to appear in the combo box or list box and adjust the column width.

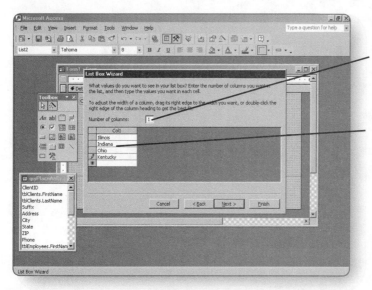

1. **Enter** the **number of columns** you need in the Number of columns text box.

2. **Type** the **values** that you want to include in each column.

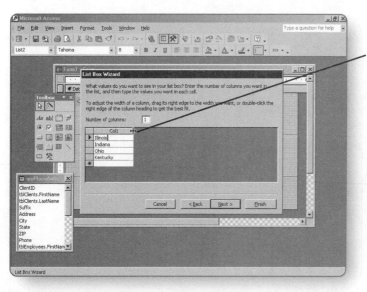

3. **Place** the **mouse pointer** on the right edge of the column that you want to adjust.

4. **Drag** the **column** to the appropriate width.

5. **Repeat Steps 3** and **4** until you adjust all necessary columns.

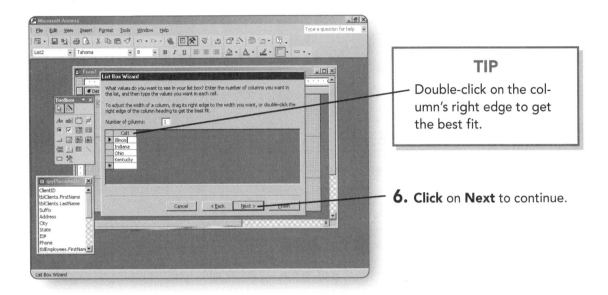

TIP

Double-click on the column's right edge to get the best fit.

6. Click on **Next** to continue.

Saving or Storing the Box Value

You can either save the combo box or list box value for future use or store it in another field.

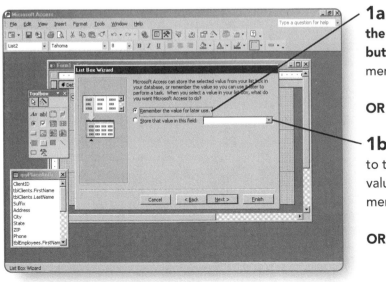

1a. Click on the **Remember the value for later use option button** to save the value in memory for future use.

OR

1b. Click on the **down arrow** to the right of the Store that value in this field text box. A menu will appear.

OR

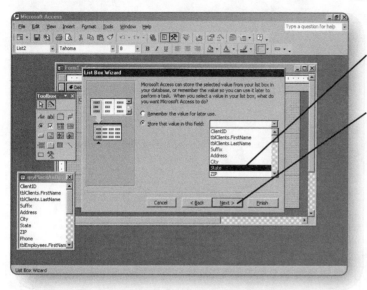

1c. Click on a **field** in which to store the box value.

2. Click on **Next** to continue.

Finishing the Combo Box or List Box

In the final wizard step, you'll create a label and specify whether to open the help window.

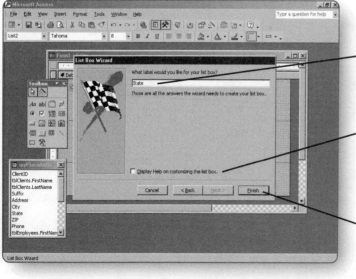

1. Enter a **name** for your combo box or list box in the text box.

2. Click on the **Display Help on customizing the combo box (or list box) check box** if you want to display a help window.

3. Click on **Finish**.

The box will appear in the form.

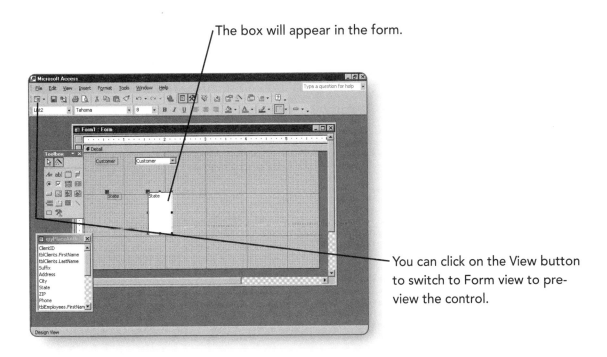

You can click on the View button to switch to Form view to pre-view the control.

If you notice in Form view that the box is too large, you can go back to Design view and resize it.

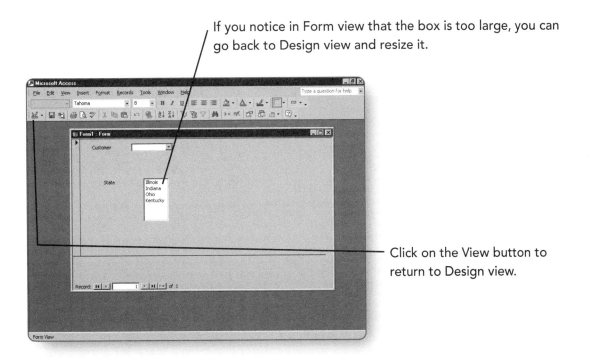

Click on the View button to return to Design view.

Part V Review Questions

1. How do you create a form that lists all fields for a single record at once? *See "Creating an AutoForm" in Chapter 15*

2. What is the difference between a Tabular AutoForm and a Datasheet AutoForm? *See "Creating an AutoForm" in Chapter 15*

3. How do you move from field to field when entering records in a form? *See "Navigating in Form View" in Chapter 16*

4. What advantages does using the Form Wizard have over creating an AutoForm? *See "Starting the Form Wizard" in Chapter 17*

5. What is the difference between a form layout and a form style? *See "Choosing a Form Layout" and "Choosing a Form Style" in Chapter 17*

6. How can you apply a different form style to a form after creating it? *See "Changing a Form's Format" in Chapter 18*

7. How would you add a field to a form after creating it? *See "Adding and Removing Fields" in Chapter 19*

8. What is the significance of the pointing finger mouse pointer versus the open hand mouse pointer when moving fields on a form? *See "Resizing a Field or Other Control" in Chapter 19*

9. Why might you want an option group on a form? *See "Adding Option Groups" in Chapter 20*

10. What is the difference between a list box and a combo box? *See "Understanding Combo and List Boxes" in Chapter 20*

PART VI

Working with Reports

21

Creating an AutoReport

You can simply and easily create basic reports using the AutoReport feature. Using AutoReport, you can automatically create both columnar and tabular reports based on a selected table or query. In this chapter, you'll learn how to:

- Create a Columnar AutoReport
- Create a Tabular AutoReport
- Save and close a report

Creating a Columnar AutoReport

You can automatically create a columnar report based on a selected table or query using the AutoReport feature. In a columnar report, one record at a time will appear on the page in a vertical format. A columnar report follows the same format as a columnar form.

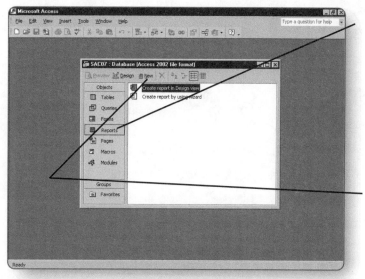

1. Click on the **Reports button** in the main database window.

2. Click on **New**. The New Report dialog box will open.

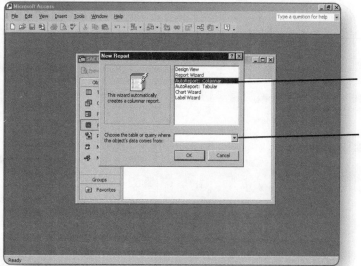

3. Click on the **AutoReport: Columnar** option.

4. Click on the **down arrow** next to the list box. A menu will appear.

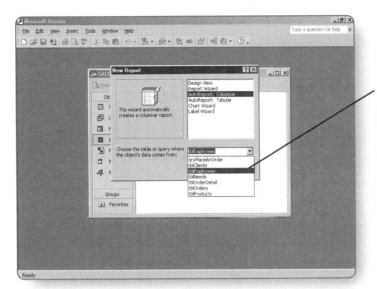

5. Click on the **table** on which you want to base your report. The table you choose will appear in the list box.

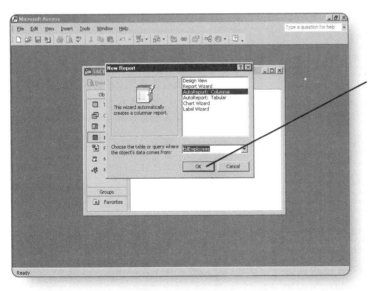

6. Click on **OK**.

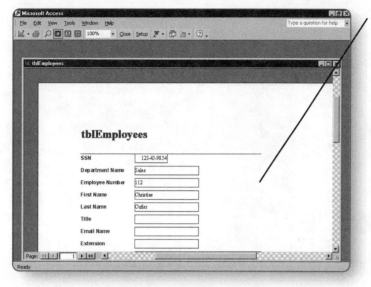

A columnar report based on the table you chose will appear in Print Preview. You can print this report as is, or you can modify its design.

NOTE

A report created using AutoReport has several defaults. It includes all fields in the table or query on which it's based. It defaults to the last AutoFormat style you used or to the Standard format if this is your first AutoReport or AutoForm. And it automatically displays in portrait orientation. If you don't want these defaults, you can later modify the report design, or you can use the Report Wizard to create your report.

Creating a Tabular AutoReport

Using the AutoReport feature, you can also create a tabular report based on a selected table or query. A tabular report displays your table data in a row and column format. Tabular reports are very similar to tabular forms.

1. Click on the **Reports tab** in the main database window.

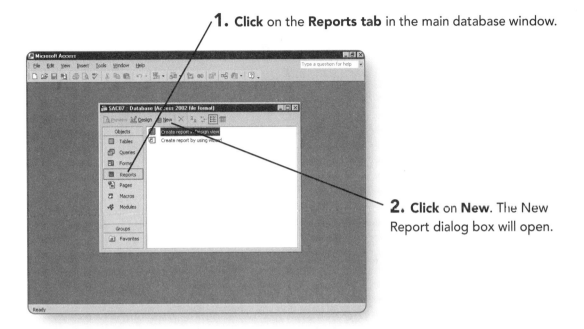

2. Click on **New**. The New Report dialog box will open.

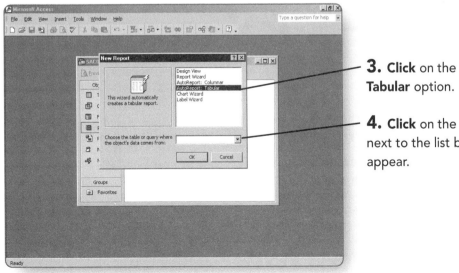

3. Click on the **AutoReport: Tabular** option.

4. Click on the **down arrow** next to the list box. A menu will appear.

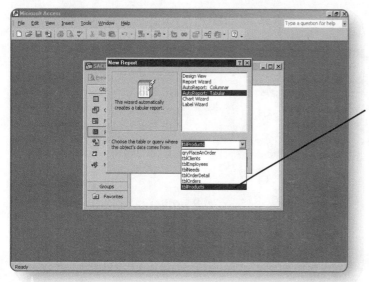

5. Click on the **table** you want. The table will appear in the list box.

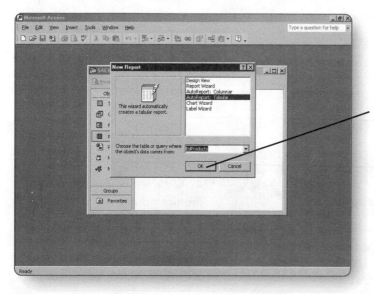

6. Click on **OK**.

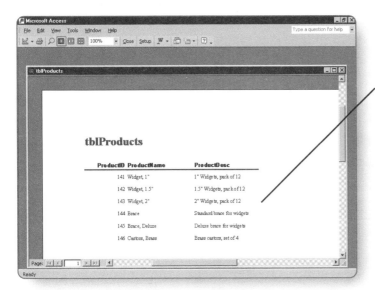

A tabular report based on this table will appear in Print Preview.

Saving and Closing a Report

After you create a report, you'll want to save it. When you close an unsaved report, Access prompts you to save it.

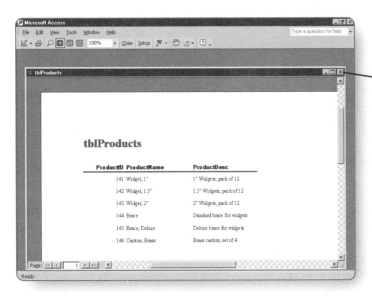

1. Click on the **Close button** for the report window. A dialog box will appear asking whether you want to save the report.

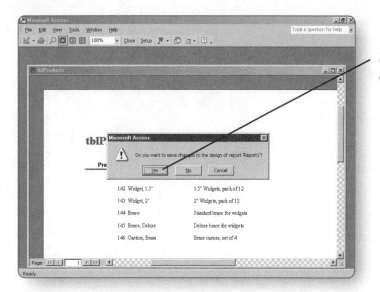

2. Click on **Yes**. The Save As dialog box will open.

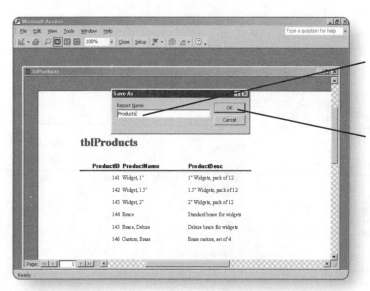

3. Enter a **name** for your report in the Report Name text box.

4. Click on **OK**. The Save As dialog box will close, and your report will be saved, but will remain open.

22

Printing Reports

You can print a report with the click of a button in Access, but the program also offers options for specifying exact report parameters. In this chapter, you'll learn how to:

- Open a report in Print Preview
- Print a default report
- Print a report with specific options

Opening a Report in Print Preview

You can open an existing report in Print Preview to see how it will look before you print.

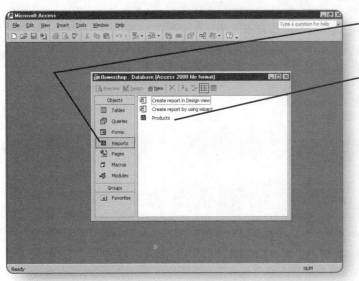

1. Click on the **Reports button** in the main database window.

2. Double-click on the **report** you want to preview. The report will open in Print Preview.

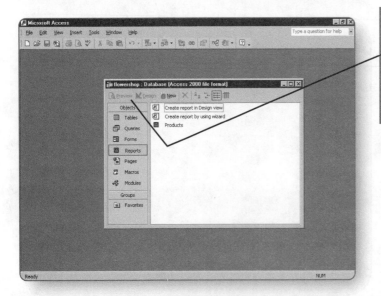

NOTE

You can also single-click on the report and then click on the Preview button.

Zooming In on a Report

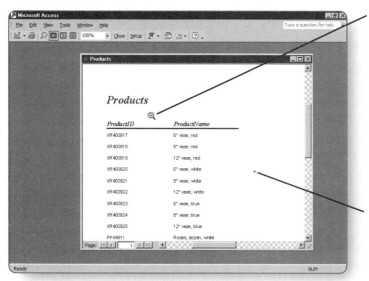

In Print Preview, the mouse pointer becomes a magnifying glass that you can use to zoom in and out of a specific area of the report for more detail. When you open a report, you will zoom in to the upper-left corner at 100%.

To display a full-page view, click anywhere on the report.

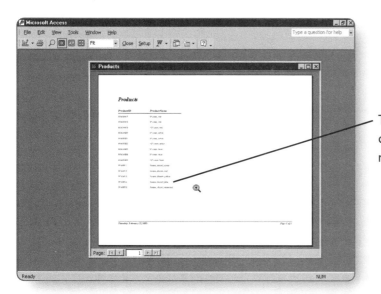

To view a particular area in more detail, click on that part of the report.

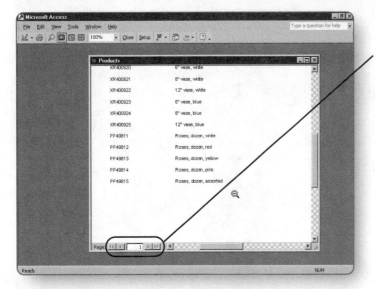

In the lower-left portion of the screen, you'll see four navigation buttons that enable you to move to the first, previous, next, or last page in the report. If the report contains only one page, as with this one, the buttons will be unavailable.

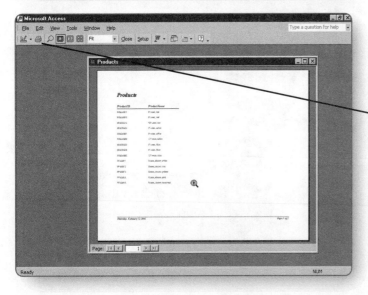

Printing a Default Report

You can quickly and easily print a report using the default settings by clicking on the Print button in Print Preview.

NOTE

The Access printing default is set to print one copy of all pages of a report using the default printer you specified in Windows.

Printing a Report with Specific Options

When you print a report, you may want to set options such as the specific pages and number of copies to print. If you have the capability to print to more than one printer, you'll want to be sure that you specify the appropriate printer.

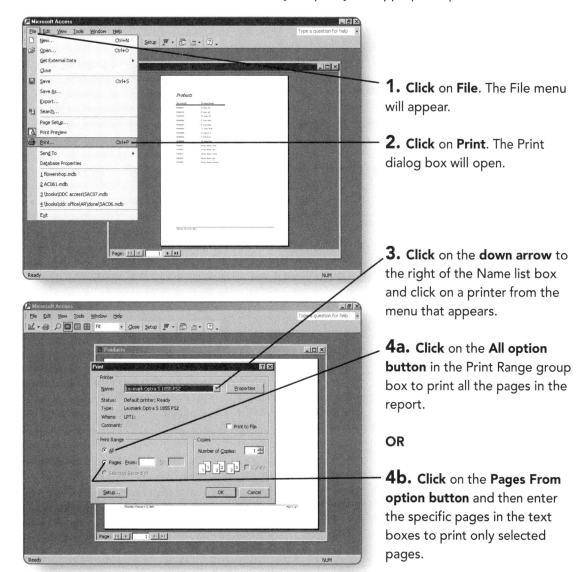

1. Click on **File**. The File menu will appear.

2. Click on **Print**. The Print dialog box will open.

3. Click on the **down arrow** to the right of the Name list box and click on a printer from the menu that appears.

4a. Click on the **All option button** in the Print Range group box to print all the pages in the report.

OR

4b. Click on the **Pages From option button** and then enter the specific pages in the text boxes to print only selected pages.

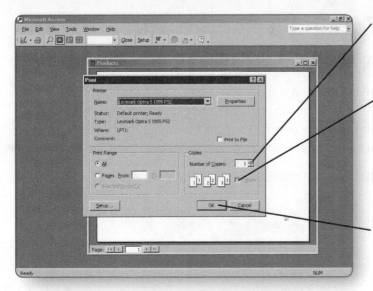

5. **Choose** the **number of copies** to print from the Number of Copies scroll box.

6. **Click** on the **Collate check box** to collate multiple copies (that is, to print sets with the pages in order). It will be unavailable (as here) if the report is only one page.

7. **Click** on **OK**. The report will print.

Setting Up Margins

You can also specify changes in the margins through the Print dialog box. Default margin settings are one inch on all sides—top, bottom, left, and right. These defaults work well in most circumstances, but if your report won't fit on a page, you might want to adjust the margins.

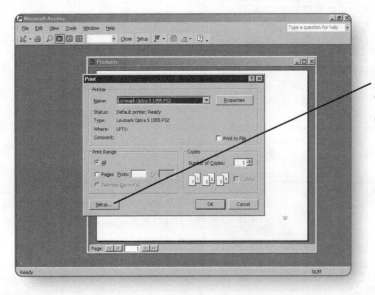

1. **Click** on the **Setup button**. The Page Setup dialog box will open.

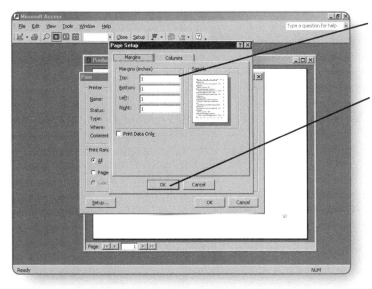

2. Enter the **desired margins** in the Margins (inches) text boxes.

3. Click on **OK**. You will return to the Print dialog box.

TIP

To change the default page orientation (portrait or landscape) before you print, choose File, Page Setup and select either the Portrait or Landscape option button on the Page tab of the Page Setup dialog box.

23

Creating a Report with the Report Wizard

Now that you know how to print reports, take a look at some other ways to create them. Using the Report Wizard, you can create a report in a matter of minutes and still have the opportunity to specify many of your own parameters. The Report Wizard lets you set grouping, sorting, and summary options, as well as choose your own style and layouts. In this chapter, you'll learn how to:

- Start the Report Wizard
- Select fields
- Create groupings and sort orders
- Specify summary options
- Specify the report layout and style
- Finish the report

Starting the Report Wizard

The Report Wizard offers step-by-step guidance on creating detailed reports, including those that contain fields from more than one table or query.

1. Click on the **Reports button** in the main database window.

2. Double-click on **Create report by using wizard** within the database window. The Report Wizard will open.

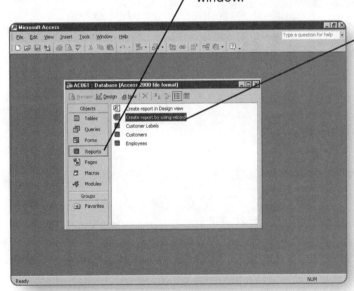

Selecting Fields

In the second step, you choose the specific fields to place in your report, including the table or query in which they are located.

1. Click on the **down arrow** to the right of the Tables/Queries list box. A menu will appear.

2. Click on the **table** or **query** from which you want to select your report fields. The table or query will appear in the list box.

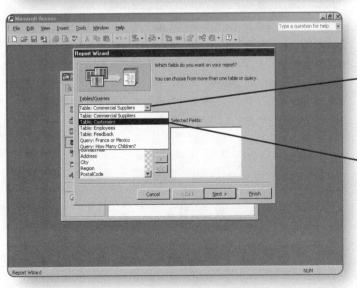

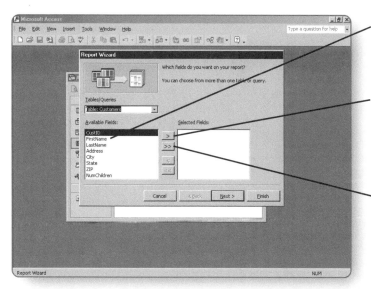

3. Choose the **first field** you want to include in your report from the Available Fields list.

4. Click on the **right arrow button**. The field will move to the Selected Fields box.

TIP

Click on the double right arrow button to include all available fields in your report.

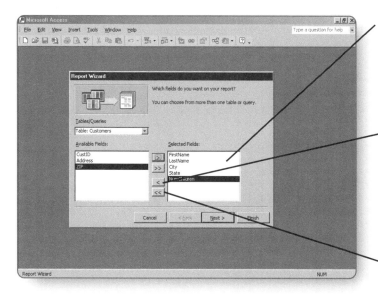

5. Repeat Steps 1 through **4** until you select all the fields you want to include in your report.

TIP

Click on the left arrow button to remove the selected field from the report.

TIP

Click on the double left arrow button to remove all fields from your report.

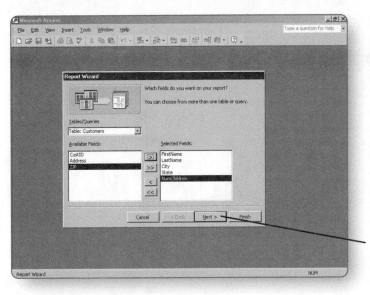

NOTE

Remember that a report can contain only a certain number of fields on one page. Consider carefully the exact information you need to include as well as the width of each field when designing a report.

6. Click on **Next**. The Report Wizard will continue to the next step.

Creating Groupings

You can create report groupings based on one or several fields.

1. Click on the **field** by which you want to group.

2. Click on the **right arrow button**. The selected field will be displayed in blue bold text in the preview box to the right.

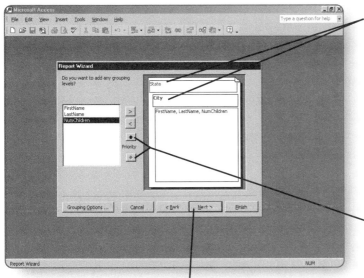

3. Repeat Steps 1 and **2** until you select all the fields on which you want to group.

> **TIP**
>
> You will probably want to group on no more than two fields for most reports.

To change the priority of the chosen grouping field, click the Up or Down arrow button.

4a. Click on **Next** to continue.

OR

4b. See the **next section** to set grouping intervals. (Do not click on Next yet.)

Setting Grouping Intervals

Access also offers the option of grouping by specified intervals. Depending on the data type of the field, the available grouping interval options will vary. For example, you might group a ZIP code field by the first three characters to separate address records into broad location categories.

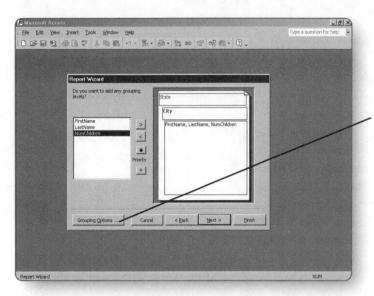

1. Click on the **Grouping Options button**. The Grouping Intervals dialog box will open.

2. Click on the **down arrow** to the right of the Grouping intervals list box. A menu will appear.

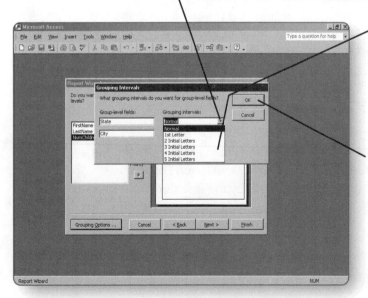

3. Click on the **interval** you want. The interval you choose will appear in the list box.

4. Repeat Steps 2 and **3** until you set all grouping intervals.

5. Click on **OK**.

NOTE

Grouping intervals are available for fields on which you've already specified a grouping level.

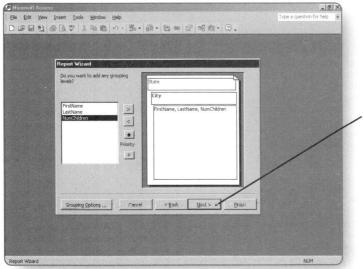

6. Click on **Next** to continue.

Specifying a Sort Order

Using the Report Wizard, you can sort up to four different fields in either ascending (the default) or descending order.

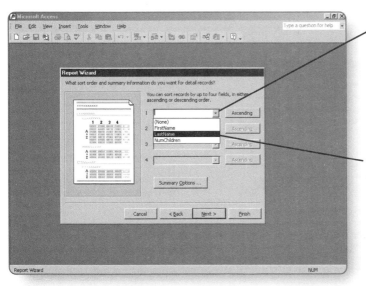

1. Click on the **down arrow** to the right of the first field list box. A menu will appear.

2. Click on the first field on which you want to sort your report. The ascending sort order will be automatically applied.

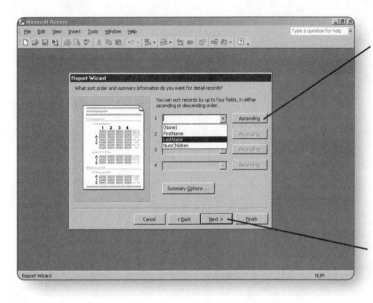

3. Click on the **Ascending button** to change the sort order to descending, if desired.

4. Repeat Steps 1, 2, and **3** until you select all sort orders.

5a. Click on **Next** to continue.

OR

5b. Continue to the **next section** to set summary options. (Do not click on Next yet.)

Specifying Summary Options

Depending on the fields you chose for your report, a Summary Options button might appear beneath the sorting options. You can use it to perform a few basic math operations (sum, average, minimum, or maximum) on a field.

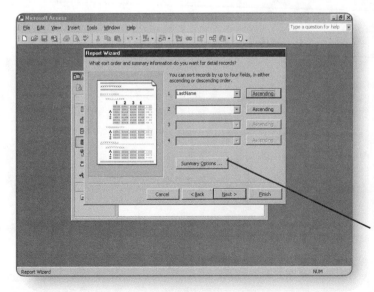

NOTE

You can continue to refine If your report contains only text fields, the Summary Options button will not appear. It appears only when the report contains at least one numeric field.

1. Click on the **Summary Options button**. The Summary Options dialog box will open.

2. Click on the **check box** for each field and summary option combination you want to include in your report.

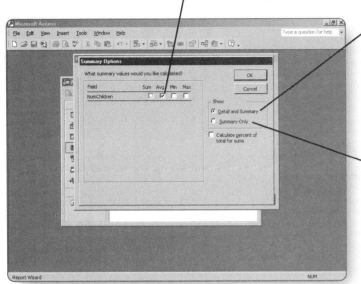

3a. Click on the **Detail and Summary option button** to display both detail and summary information in your report.

OR

3b. Click on the **Summary Only option button** to display just the summary information in the report.

4. **Click** on the **Calculate percent of total for sums check box** to display the percentage of the total this amount represents.

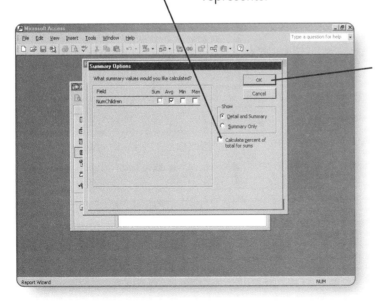

5. Click on **OK**.

Specifying the Report Layout

Next, you can choose the report layout you prefer from a selection of several different layouts. You can also set your report's orientation.

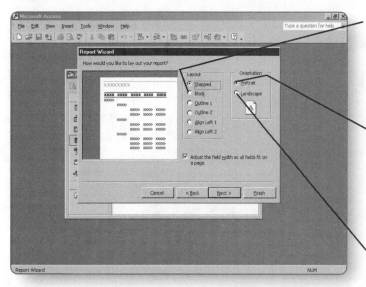

1. Click on the **layout option** you prefer in the Layout group box. A sample of the selected layout will display in the preview box.

2a. Click on the **Portrait option button** to display your report in portrait (8½ x 11) orientation.

OR

2b. Click on the **Landscape option button** to display in landscape (11 x 8½) orientation.

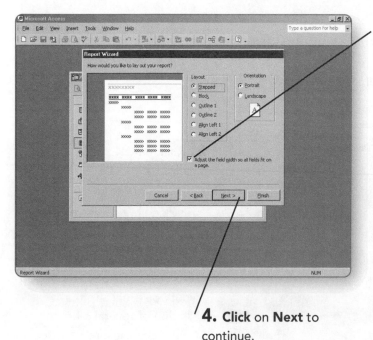

3. If you need to, **click** on the **Adjust the field width so all fields fit on a page check box**.

NOTE

By selecting the Adjust the field width so all fields fit on the page option, you will fit all of the fields on one page. However, this may truncate some fields, eliminating the characters that have been cut off.

4. Click on **Next** to continue.

Choosing a Report Style

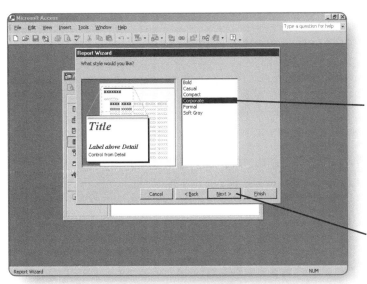

Access includes six predefined report styles, both casual and formal, from which you can choose.

1. Choose the **report style** you prefer from the list. A sample of the selected style will appear in the preview box.

2. Click on **Next** to continue.

Finishing the Report

In the final step of the Report Wizard, you'll create a report title and select the view you want to use when opening the report for the first time.

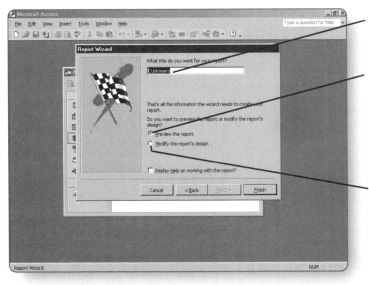

1. Enter a **name** for your report in the text box.

2a. Click on the **Preview the report option button** to open the report in Print Preview.

OR

2b. Click on the **Modify the report's design option button** to open the report in Design view.

NOTE

You can view a report in three ways: Design view, Layout Preview, and Print Preview. Design view lets you make changes to the report's design. Layout Preview gives you a basic view of the report's layout, but it doesn't include all the data. Print Preview displays your report as it will look when printed.

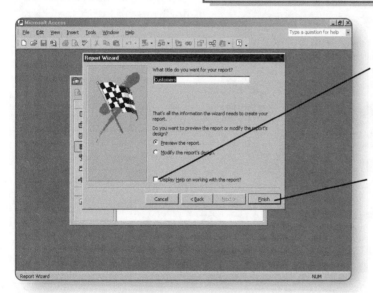

3. Click on the **Display Help on working with the report check box** if you want to display a help window when you open the report.

4. Click on Finish. The report will open based on your instructions in Step 2.

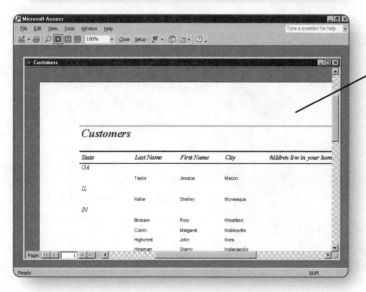

If you open your report in Print Preview, you'll see exactly how it will look on paper.

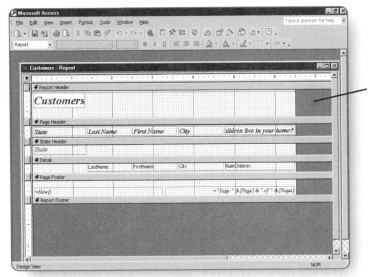

If your final report isn't exactly what you want, you can customize it in Design view, which is covered in Chapter 24, "Changing a Report's Appearance."

TIP

If you decide you want to start over again after creating a report, you can delete it by selecting it in the main database window and pressing the Delete key.

24

Changing a Report's Appearance

Once you create a report, you might want to change its default style or customize its formatting in other ways. In this chapter, you will learn how to:

- Open a report in Design view
- Change a report's format
- Modify fonts
- Bold, italicize, and underline
- Set alignment

Opening a Report in Design View

You can open an existing report in Design view to modify its design.

1. **Click** on the **Reports button** in the main database window.

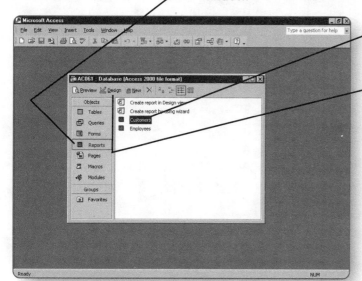

2. **Click** on the **report** you want to modify. It will be highlighted.

3. **Click** on the **Design button**. The report will open in Design view.

When you look at a report in Design view, you'll see that an Access report consists of a number of controls placed in specific report sections. Each report includes the following sections.

NOTE

You can also open a report in Design view directly from the Report Wizard by choosing the Modify the report's design option button on the final wizard step.

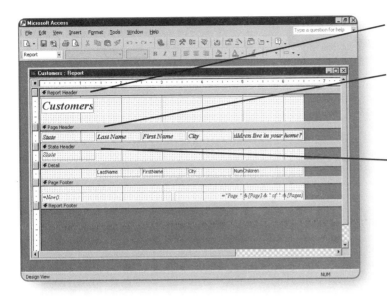

- **Report Header.** Contains the report title.

- **Page Header.** Contains information that will repeat at the top of each page, such as column labels.

- **Header for field(s).** On which you specified grouping (in the Report Wizard). Not all reports have this.

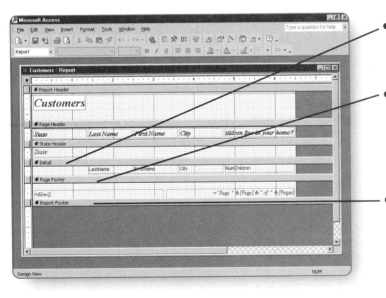

- **Detail.** The data from the chosen fields in the table or query will appear here.

- **Page Footer.** Contains information that will repeat the bottom of each page, such as the date and page number.

- **Report Footer.** Contains information to appear at the end of the report. Might be empty, as shown here.

The Report Wizard and AutoReport features automatically create report sections and place controls in the appropriate location. You can also create or modify report controls manually.

Labels appear on the report, just like on a form. You can edit these freely.

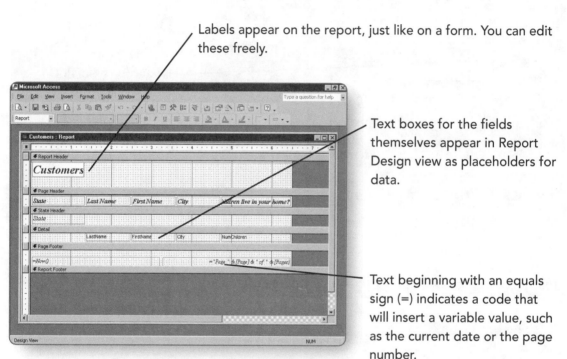

Text boxes for the fields themselves appear in Report Design view as placeholders for data.

Text beginning with an equals sign (=) indicates a code that will insert a variable value, such as the current date or the page number.

TIP

Creating report controls or making major modifications to them is an advanced feature of Access. If you're a novice user, it's usually easier to create a new report based on new report specifications than it is to make extensive modifications.

Applying an AutoFormat

When you create a report using the Report Wizard or AutoReport feature, you choose a style or AutoFormat to apply. This format uses predefined colors, borders, fonts, and font sizes designed to look good together and convey a specific image. If you don't like the AutoFormat you originally chose for your report, you can change it.

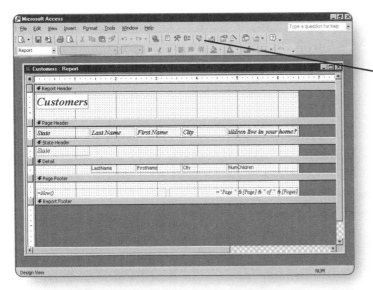

1. Click on the **AutoFormat button**. The AutoFormat dialog box will open with the current format highlighted.

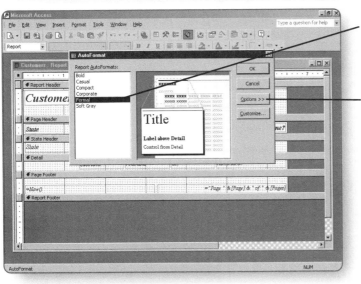

2. Click on a **new report format** in the Report AutoFormats list.

3. (Optional) **Click** on the **Options button**. The AutoFormat dialog box will extend to include the Attributes to Apply group box. All three attributes are selected by default.

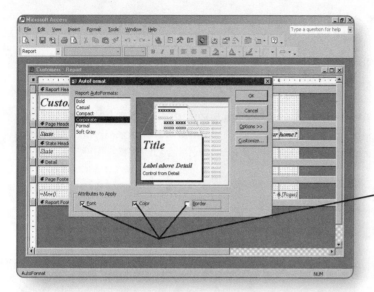

4. (Optional) **Click** on one of the **check boxes** to turn that formatting feature on or off.

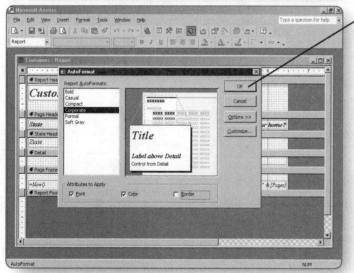

5. Click on **OK** to apply the new format.

Changing Fonts

CAUTION

Remember that Access AutoFormats and styles were designed to look good together. If you make too many font changes, your report might look muddled or be hard to read.

You can also change only the fonts in your report rather than change the entire format or style. You can change the fonts of all report controls that contain text, such as labels or text boxes.

Changing Font Style

You'll use the Font drop-down list on the Formatting toolbar to change the font style of a selected control.

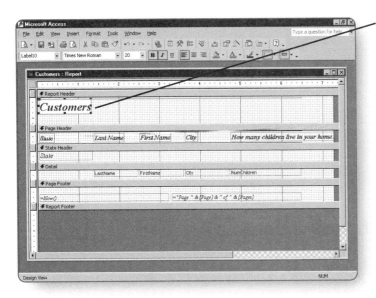

1. Click on the **control** whose font style you want to change. Handles will surround this control to indicate that it is selected.

TIP

Just like on a form, you can select more than one control by holding down Ctrl as you click on each one you want. You can then format them as a group. It's a good idea, for example, to format all the column headings in the Page Header the same way.

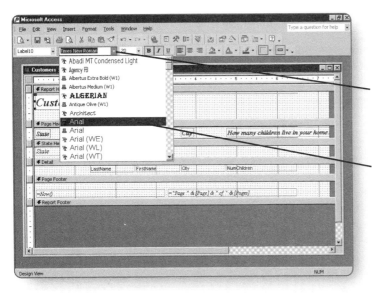

2. Click on the **down arrow** to the right of the Font drop-down list. A menu will appear.

3. Click on a **new font**. The control will appear in the new font.

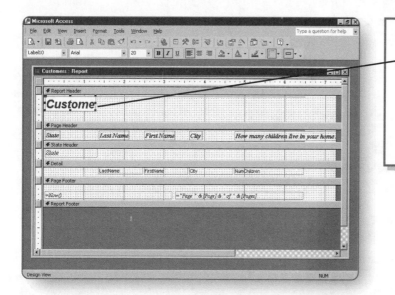

TIP

If the text appears truncated after a formatting change, double-click on a selection handle to auto-resize the frame to fit the text.

Changing Font Size

Use the Font Size drop-down list on the Formatting toolbar to modify the font size of a selected control.

1. Click on the **control** whose font size you want to change. Handles will surround this control to indicate that it is selected.

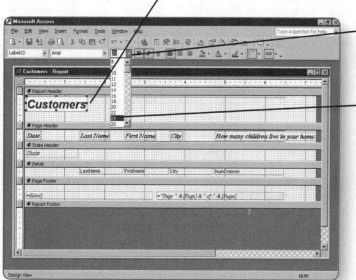

2. Click on the **down arrow** to the right of the Font Size drop-down list. A menu will appear.

3. Click on a **new font size**.

Changing Font Color

You'll use the Font/Fore Color button on the Formatting toolbar to change font color in a report.

1. Click on the **control** whose font color you want to modify. Handles will surround this control to indicate that it is selected.

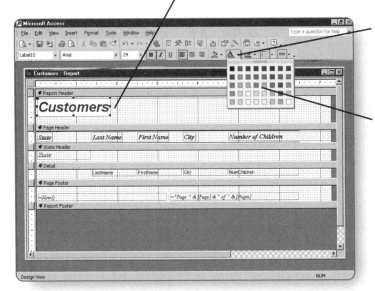

2. Click on the **down arrow** to the right of the Font/Fore Color button. The font color palette will open.

3. Click on the **color** you want to apply from the font color palette. The selected control will display in the new font color.

TIP

Click on the Font/Fore Color button's face, rather than the arrow next to the button, to apply the default color that appears on the button.

Bolding, Italicizing, and Underlining

In addition to changing the actual fonts in your report, you can modify them by bolding, italicizing, and underlining. These features are particularly useful when you want to emphasize something in your report. You can bold, italicize, and underline any control that includes text, such as a label or text box.

1. Click on the **control** that you want to bold. It will be selected.

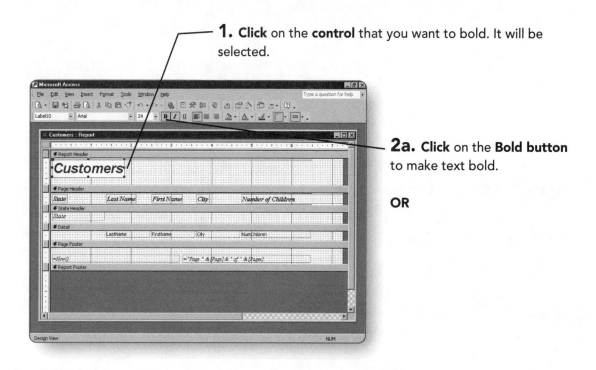

2a. Click on the **Bold button** to make text bold.

OR

2b. Click on the **Italic button** to make text italicized.

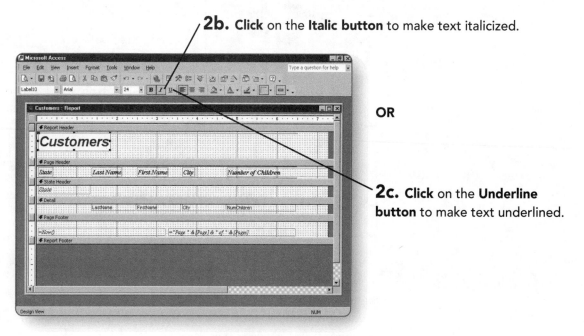

OR

2c. Click on the **Underline button** to make text underlined.

Setting Alignment

You can set left, center, and right alignment on your Access reports using buttons on the Formatting toolbar.

1. Click on the **control** whose alignment you want to change.

2a. Click on the **Align Left button** to left-align the text.

OR

2b. Click on the **Center button** to center selected text.

OR

2c. Click on the **Align Right button** to right-align the text. The text will be aligned according to your instructions in Step 2.

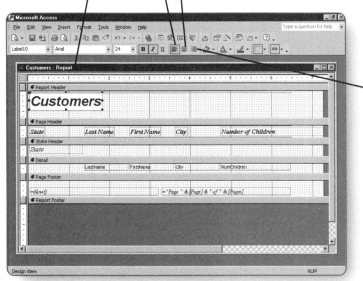

TIP

Many of the skills you learned for formatting forms in Chapters 18 and 19 also apply to formatting reports. You can add fields, add labels, and so on. Experiment on your own with report formatting. If you make a mistake, use the Report Wizard (refer to Chapter 23, " Creating a Report with the Report Wizard") to re-create the form and start over.

25

Creating Mailing Labels

One of the handiest report types in Access is the Mailing Label report. Access provides a Label Wizard that walks you through the process painlessly. In this chapter, you will learn how to:

- Start the Label Wizard
- Select the label type
- Format the labels
- Choose fields to include on the labels

Starting the Label Wizard

The Label Wizard does not have a shortcut on the Reports list, so you must start it from the New Report dialog box.

1. Click on the **Reports button** in the main database window. A list of existing reports will appear.

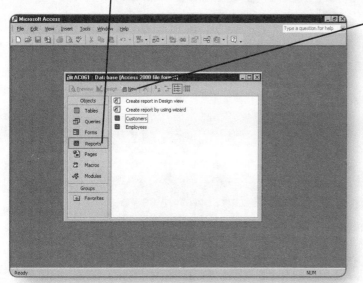

2. Click on the **New button.** The New Report dialog box will open.

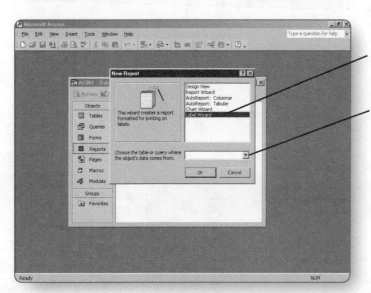

3. Click on **Label Wizard**. Label Wizard will be selected.

4. Click on the **down arrow**. A list of tables and queries will appear.

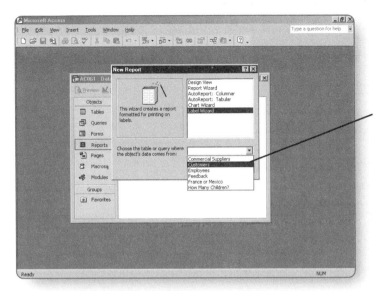

5. Click on the **table or query** on which you want to base the labels. The name will appear in the box.

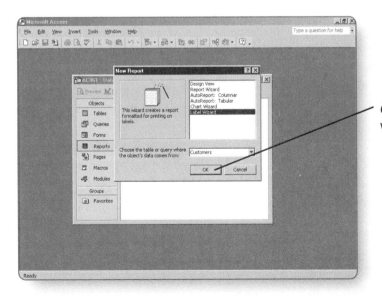

6. Click on **OK**. The Label Wizard will start.

Selecting the Label Size and Type

Your first task is to tell the Label Wizard what kind of labels you want to print on. There are many label manufacturers, and each one makes many different sizes.

1a. **Locate** the **manufacturer name** and **model number** for your labels.

OR

1b. If that information is not available, **measure a label** and **count** the number of **rows and columns** of labels per sheet.

<table>
<tr><td>

CAUTION

If you have a laser printer, make sure the labels you buy are specifically designed for laser printers. If you use labels designed for an ink-jet printer in a laser printer, they can melt, causing great damage to the printer.

</td></tr>
</table>

2. Click on **English** or **Metric**, depending on how your labels are measured.

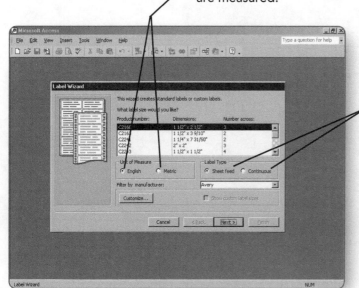

English measurements are in inches ("); Metric measurements are in millimeters (mm).

3. Click on **Sheet feed** or **Continuous,** depending on the label sheet type.

Sheet fed labels are individual sheets; Continuous means each page is joined to the next at top and bottom.

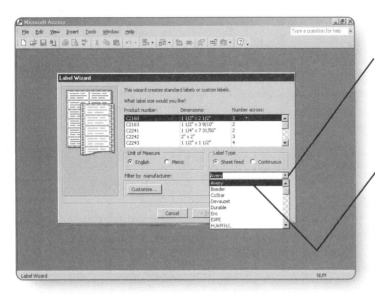

4. Click on the **down arrow** next to Filter by manufacturer. A list of manufacturers will appear.

5. Click on the **manufacturer** of your labels. The manufacturer's label model numbers will appear on the Product number list.

TIP

If you are not sure about the manufacturer or if your manufacturer does not appear, choose Avery. Avery is the most popular label manufacturer, and you can probably find an Avery type that matches the labels you have.

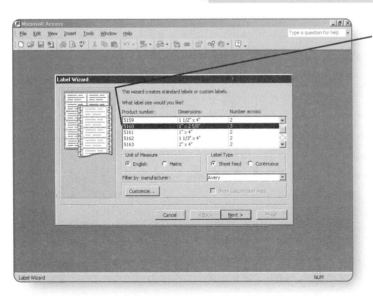

6. Click on the **model number** of your labels. The model will appear highlighted.

TIP

If you do not know the model number, pick a model that matches your labels in both label size and number of columns per sheet.

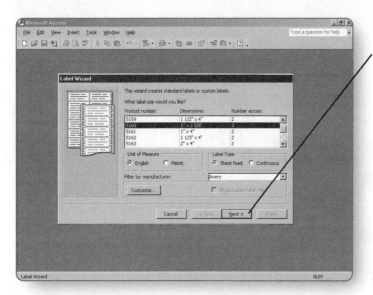

7. Click on **Next.** The Wizard will next ask you about text font and size for the label.

Formatting the Label Text

The Label Wizard prompts you to specify the font, size, and text attributes you want to use for your labels.

TIP

Do not use a large font size on a small label, or the text will be truncated. In most cases, 8-point text is large enough for mailing. Arial is one of the best fonts for mailing because it is easy to read and very clear even at small sizes.

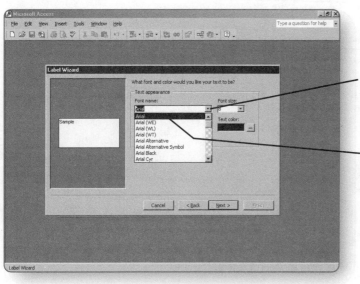

1. Click on the **down arrow** next to **Font name.** A list of fonts will appear.

2. Click on the **font** you want to use. Its name will appear in the Font name box.

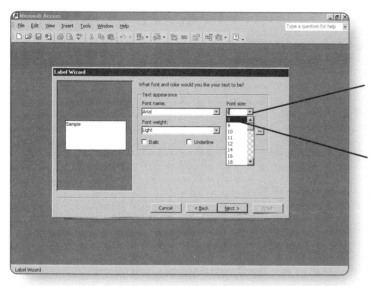

3. Click on the **down arrow** next to **Font size**. A list of font sizes will appear.

4. Click on the **font size** you want. Its number will appear in the Font size box.

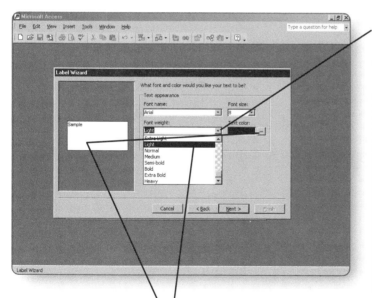

5. Click on the **down arrow** next to **Font weight**. A list of font weights will appear.

NOTE

The font weight is the measure of how thick the letters will be. Certain fonts come in various weights, such as Light, Normal, Bold, and Heavy. Light or Normal weights are usually best for small labels.

---

6. Click on the **font weight** you want. Its name will appear in the Font weight box.

7. Click on the **Text color** button. The Color dialog box will open.

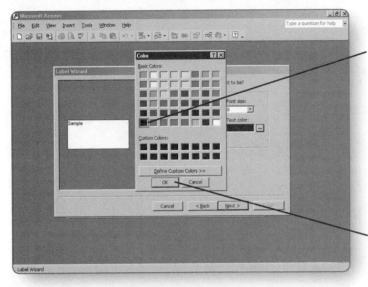

8. **Click** on the **color** you want for the text.

TIP

Choose a dark color for best results on white labels.

---

9. **Click** on **OK**. The selected color will appear in the Text color box.

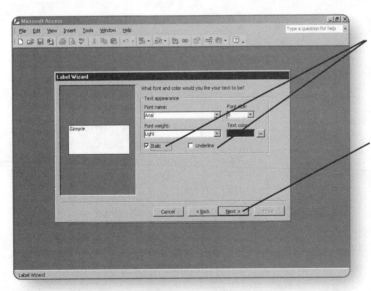

10. **Click** on the **Underline** and **Italic check boxes** to choose those attributes if desired.

11. **Click** on **Next**. The Label Wizard will prompt you to choose fields for the label.

Choosing and Arranging Label Fields

Next, you will construct your label by selecting fields from the chosen table or query and specifying where they will appear on each label.

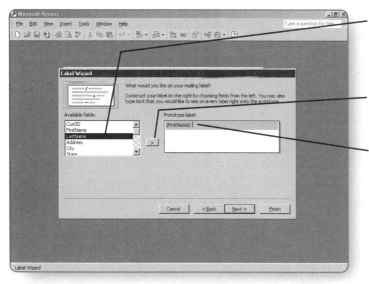

1. **Click** on a **field** that you want to appear on the label. It will be highlighted.

2. **Click** on the **right arrow button**.

The field will appear in the Prototype label area.

3. **Add** any **punctuation**, **spaces**, or **paragraph breaks** needed between the field just added and the next one.

NOTE

For example, press Enter to start a new line. You will need a space between two fields on the same line, such as FirstName and LastName. You might also need punctuation such as a comma (and space) between the City and State fields.

---

4. **Repeat Steps 1** through **3** to add more fields to the label.

Here are the suggested fields for a standard mailing label:

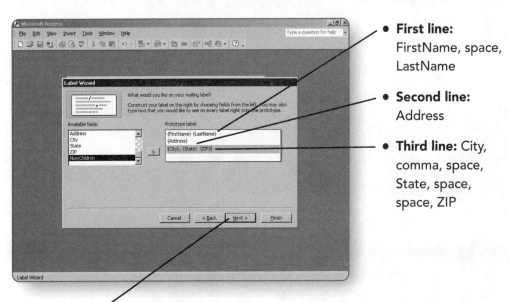

- **First line:** FirstName, space, LastName

- **Second line:** Address

- **Third line:** City, comma, space, State, space, space, ZIP

5. Click on **Next** to continue. The Label Wizard will next prompt you for a sort order.

Setting the Sort Order for Records

Next, the Wizard asks whether you want to sort the labels in any particular order. You might find it useful to sort them by LastName, for example; and some mass mailing services require that mailings be sorted by ZIP code. The sort fields you choose after the first one take effect only in event of a "tie" in the first sort field. For example, if you choose LastName and then FirstName, only records that have the same last name will be sorted by first name.

1. Click on a **field to sort by**. The field will be selected.

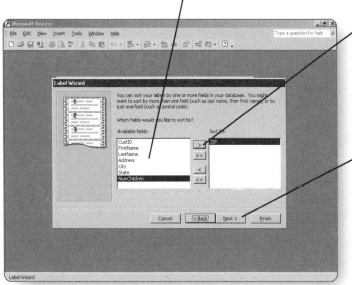

2. Click on the **right arrow button**. The field will appear on the Sort by list.

3. Repeat Steps 1 and **2** to choose more fields if desired.

4. Click on **Next** to continue.

Finishing the Label Wizard

As the last step of the Label Wizard, you specify a name for the report and open it either in Preview or Design view.

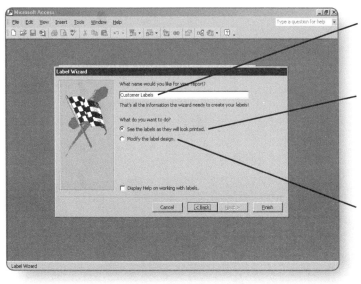

1. Type a **name** for the label report. The name will appear in the text box.

2a. Click on **See the labels as they will look printed** if you want to preview the labels.

OR

2b. Click on **Modify the label design** if you want to change the labels in Report Design view.

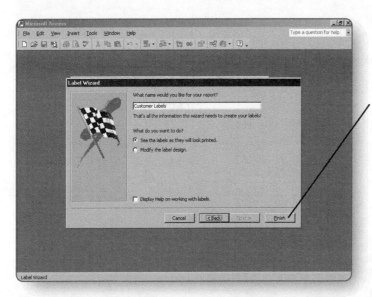

3. Click on **Finish**. Your labels will appear in Preview, or your report will open in Design view, depending on your selection in Step 2.

NOTE

You can work with a label report the same as you do with any other report. See Chapter 22, "Printing Reports," for help printing a report.

Part VI Review Questions

1. What are the two sort orders, and how does each one sort? *See "Sorting Data" in Chapter 11*

2. How can you filter your table data based on more than one criterion? *See "Filtering Data" in Chapter 11*

3. How can you quickly find a specific word in a table that contains thousands of records? *See "Finding Data" in Chapter 11*

4. What options does a summary query offer? *See "Choosing a Detail or Summary Query" in Chapter 12*

5. What information appears in the top part of the Query Design window? *See "Starting a Query in Design View" in Chapter 13*

6. How do you delete a field from a query? *See "Deleting Fields" in Chapter 13*

7. In which row of the query design grid do you enter criteria? *See "Specifying Criteria" in Chapter 14*

8. If you want to enter two criteria and include all records that match either one, where do you enter the second criterion? *See "Using OR Criteria" in Chapter 14*

9. What button do you click on to make the Total line display in the query design grid? *See "Specifying Calculations" in Chapter 14*

10. What calculation does the Group By entry in the Total line perform? *See "Specifying Calculations" in Chapter 14*

PART VII

Working with the Web

26

Adding Hyperlinks

Access includes the powerful capability of linking data in tables and forms to documents on the Internet, your company's network, or your own computer hard drive through the use of *hyperlinks*. In this chapter, you will learn how to:

- Add hyperlinks to a table in Design view
- Add a hyperlink column in Datasheet view
- Enter hyperlinks in tables
- Test your hyperlinks
- Add a hyperlink label to a form

Adding Hyperlinks to a Table in Design View

You can include hyperlinks to the following:

- Documents on the Internet, such as a World Wide Web page

- Documents on your company network's intranet site (internal Internet)

- Documents on your own computer's hard drive, such as other Office XP files

For example, in a table that stores customer information, you might want to include a field that links to each customer's Web site. You can add a hyperlink field to a table in Design view.

1. **Click** on the **Tables button** in the main database window.

2. **Click** on the **table** that you want to open. It will be highlighted.

3. **Click** on the **Design button**. The table will open in Design view.

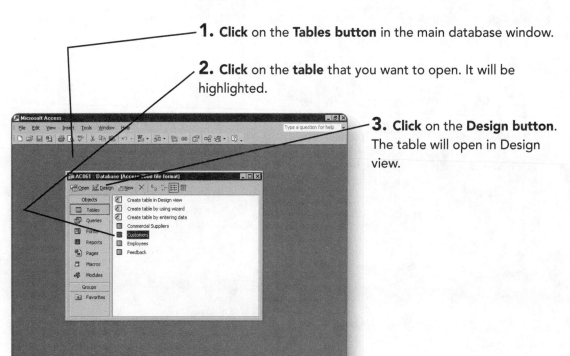

4. Move the **insertion point** to a blank row by doing one of the following:

- Click in the first empty row of the grid.

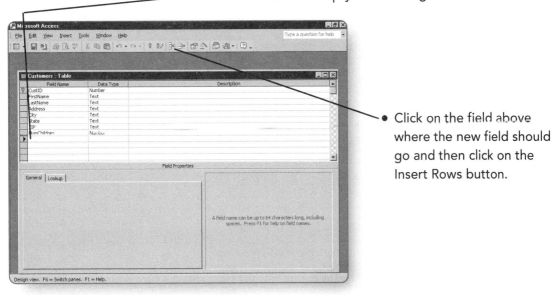

- Click on the field above where the new field should go and then click on the Insert Rows button.

5. Enter the **name** for the new field in the Field Name column.

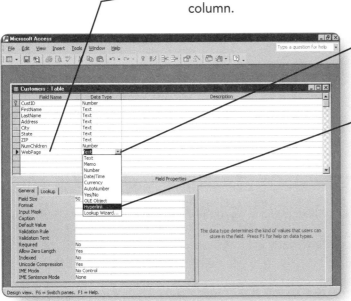

6. Click on the **down arrow** to the left of the Data Type column. A menu will appear.

7. Click on **Hyperlink** as the new data type.

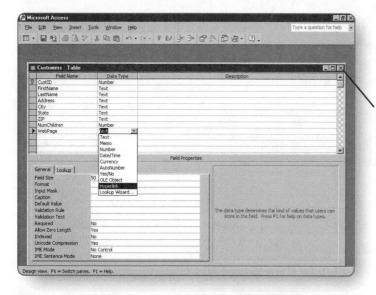

8. Click on the **Close button**. A dialog box will ask if you want to save changes.

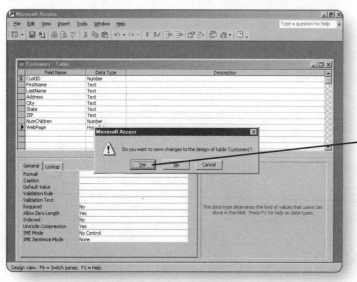

9. Click on **Yes**. The changes will be saved, and the table will close.

Adding Hyperlink Columns in Datasheet View

If you are already in Datasheet view, you can add a hyperlink column directly to the table datasheet.

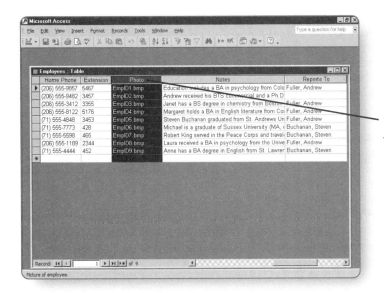

1. Select the **field column** to the right of where you want to insert the hyperlink column.

2. Click on **Insert**. The Insert drop-down menu will appear.

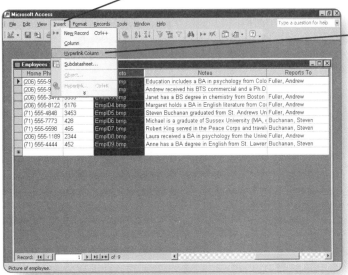

3. Click on **Hyperlink Column**. A hyperlink field will be inserted to the left of the selected column.

When you save the changes, the new field will automatically be saved with the Hyperlink data type.

NOTE

If you use this shortcut method to add a hyperlink column, you must rename the column and then set any additional properties in Design view.

Entering Hyperlinks in Tables

After you add a hyperlink field to a table—either in Design view or Datasheet view—you can enter the actual hyperlinks in Datasheet view. The most common types of hyperlinks you'll include in a table are links to Web pages or e-mail addresses. For example, you could add fields to a Customers table that list a customer's Web page and e-mail address.

A hyperlink that you store in an Access table can have up to four parts:

- **Display text**. The text you want to display in your hyperlink field. This is usually the name of the Web site.

- **Address**. The URL of the site to which you want to link; http://www.microsoft.com is an example of an address.

> ### NOTE
> URL refers to *Uniform Resource Locator,* the address of the Internet document, Web page, or object to which you want to link. It includes the protocol, such as http, as well the exact address location.

- **Subaddress**. The exact location in the document or page to which you are linking. This is particularly useful when you are linking to another document on your computer, such as another Office file. The subaddress could be a bookmark name in Word or a slide number in PowerPoint, for example.

- **ScreenTip**. The text you want to display when you place the mouse pointer over a hyperlink. A ScreenTip is handy, for example, when you want to use a hyperlink to link to another Access object and need to provide directions on what the link does, such as "Click here to enter order information."

Access requires the following format when entering a hyperlink: displaytext#address#subaddress#screentip. The address is required for a hyperlink field to work properly; the display text, subaddress, and ScreenTip are optional. You can manually type the text like that, or you can use the Insert Hyperlink dialog box to help you.

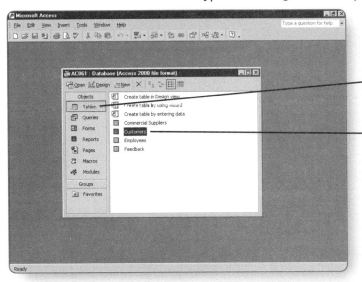

1. Click on the **Tables button** in the main database window.

2. Double-click on the **table you want to open**. The table will open in Datasheet view.

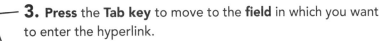

3. Press the **Tab key** to move to the **field** in which you want to enter the hyperlink.

4. Click on the **Insert Hyperlink button**. The Insert Hyperlink dialog box will open.

In this dialog box, you can create several types of hyperlinks, including those to existing Web pages or e-mail addresses, two of the most common types of hyperlinks in tables.

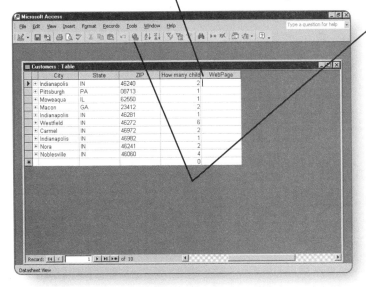

5a. See the next section, **"Linking to a Web Page,"** to create a hyperlink to a Web address.

OR

5b. See the section **"Linking to an E-Mail Address"** to create a hyperlink to an e-mail address.

Linking to a Web Page

> ### NOTE
>
> If you just want to enter a URL without display text or a ScreenTip, you can type the URL directly into the field in Datasheet view.

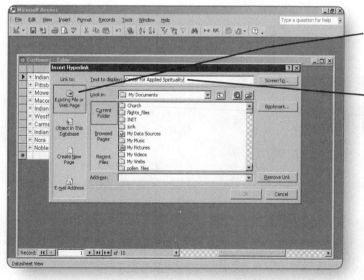

1. Click on the **Existing File or Web Page button**.

2. (Optional) **Enter** the **display text** you want to appear in the field, if any, in the Text to display box.

If you enter nothing here, the URL that you enter in Step 3 will appear in the field.

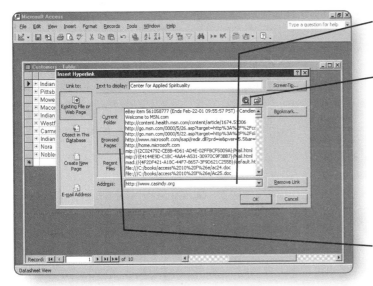

3. Enter the **URL** in the Address text box.

If you don't know the page's exact address, click on the Browse the Web button. This opens your Web browser. Display the page there and then return to Access using the taskbar; the address will be filled in for you automatically.

You can also click on the Browsed Pages button to list Web sites you have recently visited with your browser and then click on one of them to select it.

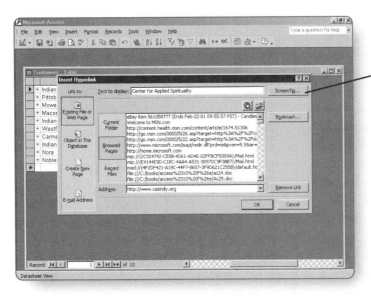

4. Click on the **ScreenTip button** if you want to add a ScreenTip. The Set Hyperlink ScreenTip dialog box will open.

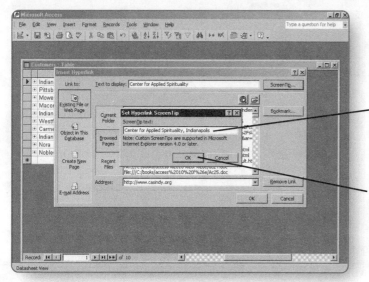

5. Enter the **text** you want to appear as a ScreenTip in the ScreenTip text box.

6. Click on **OK** to return to the Insert Hyperlink dialog box.

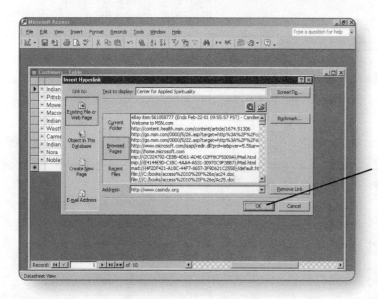

7. Click on **OK**. The hyperlink will appear in the field.

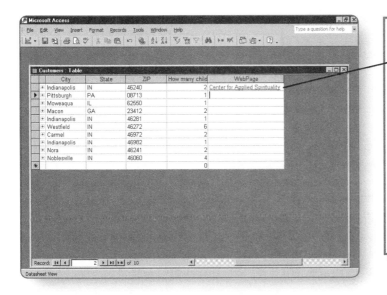

Linking to an E-Mail Address

You can also link to an e-mail address from within the Insert Hyperlink dialog box. This type of hyperlink enables you to address an e-mail message to the person by clicking on the hyperlink. Your default e-mail program opens when you click on the hyperlink to handle the mail operation.

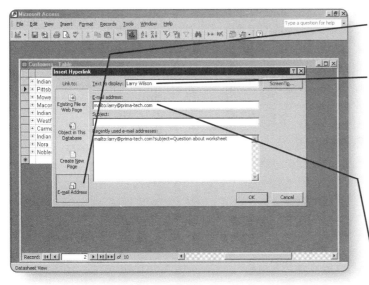

1. Click on the **E-mail Address button**.

2. Enter the **display text** that you want to appear in the field, if any, in the Text to display text box.

If you enter nothing here, the actual e-mail address will display.

3. Enter the **e-mail address** in the E-mail address text box.

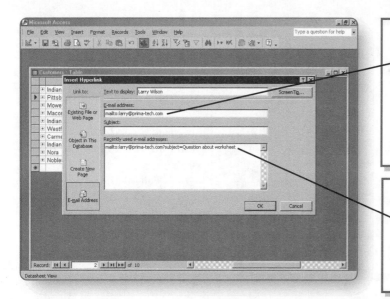

NOTE

As soon as you enter an e-mail address, it is automatically prefaced by the phrase mailto. This phrase is required to send an e-mail.

TIP

You can also select an e-mail address from the Recently used e-mail addresses list.

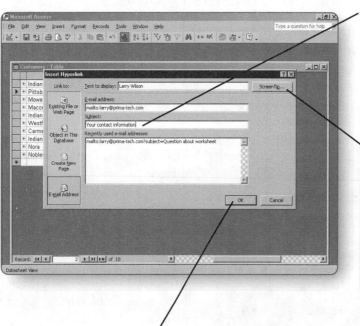

4. (Optional) **Enter** the **text** you want to automatically appear in the subject of your e-mail message in the Subject text box.

TIP

You can also include a ScreenTip by clicking on the ScreenTip button and entering a ScreenTip in the Set Hyperlink ScreenTip dialog box, just as you learned to do for a URL in the preceding section.

5. Click on **OK** to return to Datasheet view.

TIP

If you just want to enter an e-mail address without display text or a ScreenTip, you can type the address directly into the field in Datasheet view.

Testing Your Hyperlink

To verify whether a hyperlink you've created works properly, you should test it.

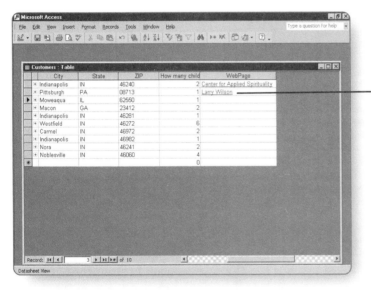

To test a hyperlink, click on it.

Your default browser will open and display the linked document or Web page, or your e-mail program will open with a new message ready to send to the e-mail recipient.

Adding a Hyperlink Label to a Form

Hyperlinks are very versatile. Besides referring to a URL or e-mail address, you can also refer to another object within your database. For example, you can create a hyperlink on a form that links to another form so that users can click on that hyperlink to jump to the other form.

1. Click on the **Forms button** in the main database window.

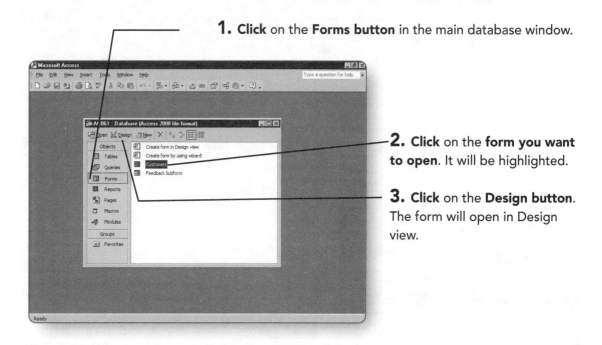

2. Click on the **form you want to open**. It will be highlighted.

3. Click on the **Design button**. The form will open in Design view.

4. Click on the **section of the form** where you want to place the hyperlink.

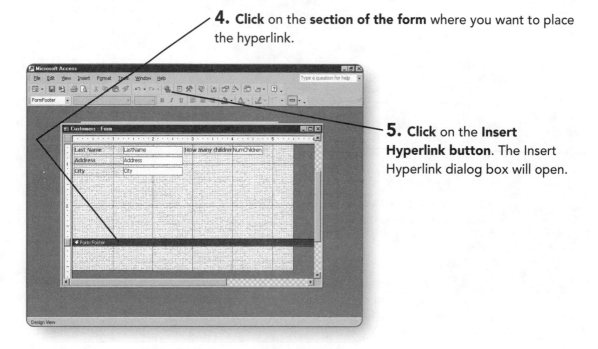

5. Click on the **Insert Hyperlink button**. The Insert Hyperlink dialog box will open.

6. **Click** on the **Object in This Database button**.

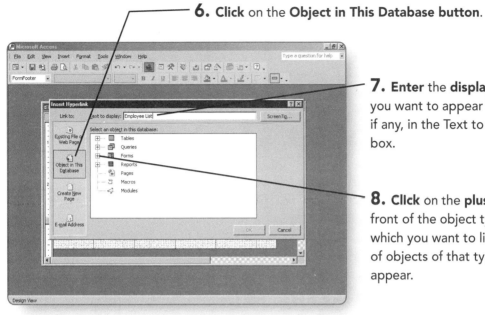

7. **Enter** the **display text** that you want to appear in the field, if any, in the Text to display text box.

8. **Click** on the **plus sign** in front of the object type to which you want to link. A list of objects of that type will appear.

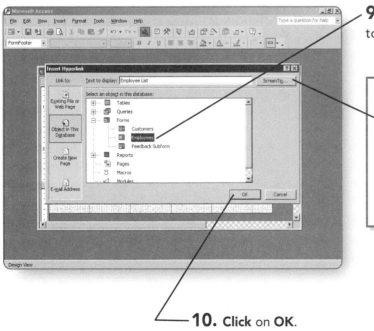

9. **Click** on the **specific object** to which you want to link.

TIP

You can also include a ScreenTip by clicking on the ScreenTip button and entering a ScreenTip in the Set Hyperlink ScreenTip dialog box.

10. **Click** on **OK**.

The hyperlink will appear in the upper-left corner of the section you chose in Step 4, and you can then drag the hyperlink wherever you want it.

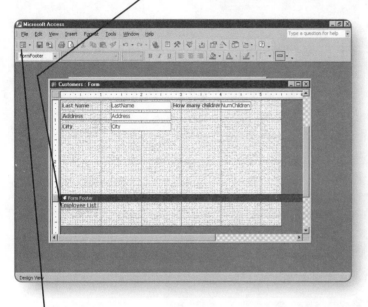

Click on the View button to preview the form in Form view. When you click on the hyperlink, you will jump to the other form.

27

Creating Data Access Pages

Access includes an object called a *data access page* that enables users to view and access your Access databases via the Web. Using the AutoPage or Page Wizard features, you can quickly create a page, specify options such as sort order and theme, and then preview your work via a browser. In this chapter, you'll learn how to:

- Understand data access pages
- Create a columnar AutoPage
- Create a data access page with the Page Wizard
- Preview a data access page

Understanding Data Access Pages

A data access page is very similar to a form or report, except that it functions as a Web page. A user can open your data access page from either the Internet or an internal company intranet. You can create data access pages to view, analyze, and report on information or to serve as a method of data entry. In the latter case, you could potentially have multiple users updating table information over the Internet. You'll most likely use data access pages if you create multi-user Access databases and already have a Web or intranet site on which to place the pages.

CAUTION

You must have Microsoft Internet Explorer 5.0 or higher installed on your system to fully make use of the data access page capabilities. Version 5.5 was probably installed when you installed Office XP, but you can check by choosing Help, About Internet Explorer from within Internet Explorer to see the version number.

Creating a Columnar AutoPage

As with other Access objects (such as AutoForm and AutoReport), an AutoPage is the simplest form of a data access page. You can automatically create a columnar page based on a selected table or query using the AutoPage feature. In a columnar page, one record will appear on the page at a time, in a vertical format. A columnar page follows the same format as a columnar form or report.

1. Click on the **Pages button** in the main database window.

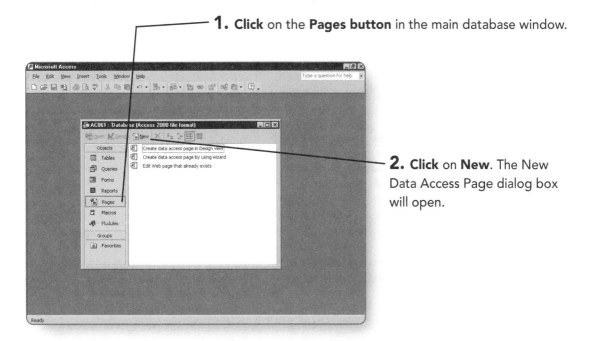

2. Click on **New**. The New Data Access Page dialog box will open.

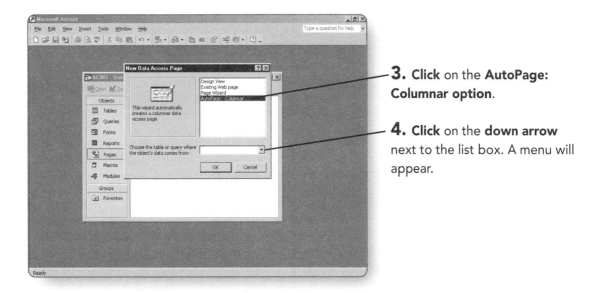

3. Click on the **AutoPage: Columnar option**.

4. Click on the **down arrow** next to the list box. A menu will appear.

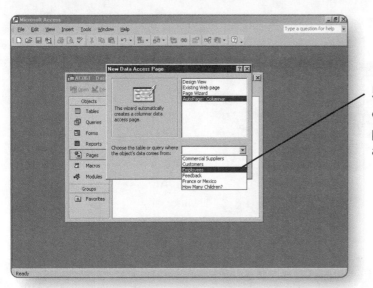

5. Click on the **table or query** on which you want to base your page. The table or query will appear in the list box.

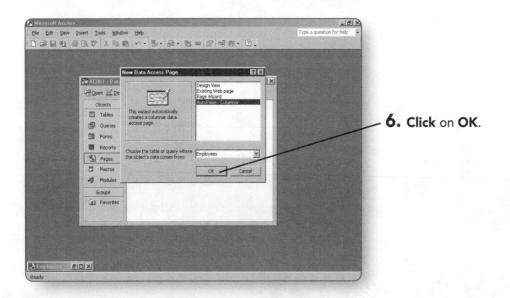

6. Click on **OK**.

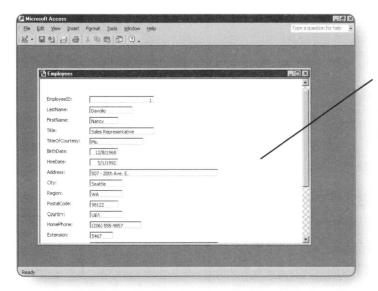

A columnar page based on this table will appear in Page view. You can later modify its design in Design view, if desired.

Creating a Page with the Page Wizard

The Page Wizard offers step-by-step guidance on creating detailed data access pages, including those that contain fields from more than one table or query.

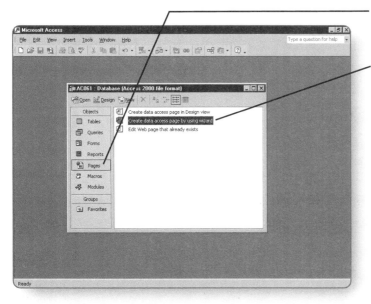

1. **Click** on the **Pages button** in the main database window.

2. **Double-click** on **Create data access page by using wizard** within the database window. The Page Wizard will open.

Selecting Fields

In the second step, you choose the specific fields to place in your page, including the table or query in which they are located.

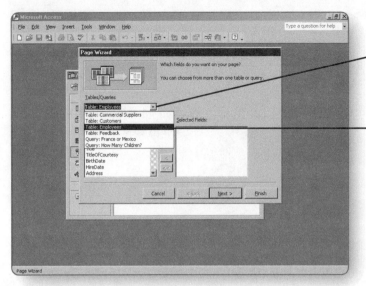

1. **Click** on the **down arrow** to the right of the Tables/Queries list box. A menu will appear.

2. **Click** on the **table or query** from which you want to select your page field. A list of the fields for that table/query will appear in the Available Fields list box.

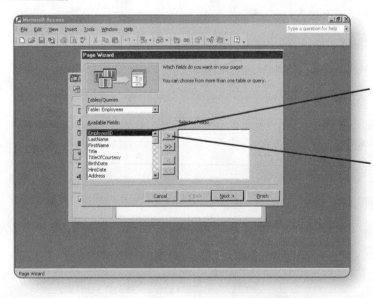

3. **Choose** the **first field** you want to include in your page from the Available Fields list.

4. **Click** on the **right arrow button**. The field will move to the Selected Fields list.

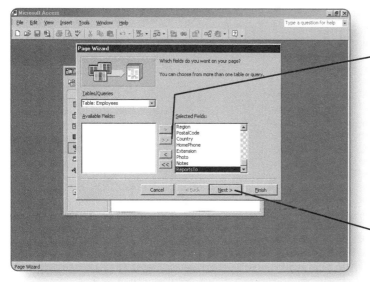

TIP

Click on the double right arrow button to include all available fields in your page.

5. Repeat Steps 1 through **4** until you select all the fields you want to include in your page.

6. Click on **Next**. The Page Wizard will continue to the next step.

Creating Groupings

Just like with reports, you can create page groupings based on one or several fields.

CAUTION

Creating groupings on a data access page makes the page read-only. If you create groupings, users will be able to view the page, but they won't be able to enter data.

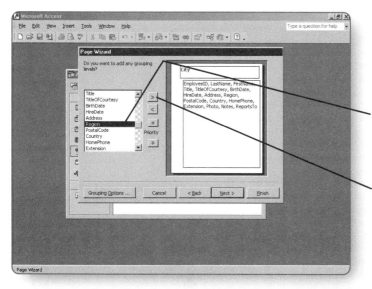

1. Click on the **field** on which you want to group from the list of available fields.

2. Click on the **right arrow button**. The selected field will display in blue, bold text in the preview box to the right.

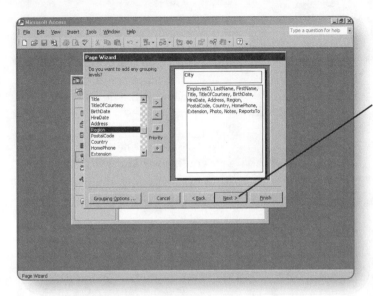

3. Repeat Steps 1 and **2** until you select all the fields on which you want to group.

4a. Click on **Next** to continue.

OR

4b. See the **next section** to change the priority among multiple fields by which you are grouping.

> ### TIP
>
> To remove a field grouping, click on the field name and then click on the left arrow button.

Changing the Grouping Priority

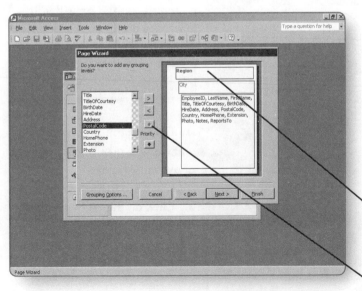

In the preview window, the grouping level fields display in blue bold text and are listed in order of grouping priority, with each subsequent level slightly indented. The order is based on the order in which you specify grouping levels, but you can easily change it.

1. Click on the **grouping field** in the preview box whose priority you want to change.

2a. Click on the **up arrow button** to move this field to a higher priority.

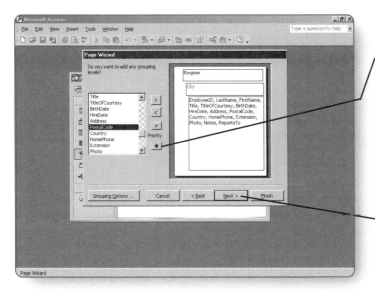

OR

2b. **Click** on the **down arrow button** to move this field to a lower priority.

3. Repeat Steps 1 and **2** until you've changed the grouping priorities to the desired order.

4a. **Click** on **Next** to continue.

OR

4b. See the **next section** to set grouping intervals.

Setting Grouping Intervals

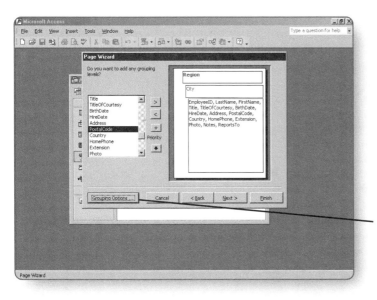

Access also offers the option of grouping by specified intervals. Depending on the data type of the field, the available grouping interval options will vary. For example, number fields include grouping options in several different multiples, and text fields include grouping options based on letter.

1. Click on the **Grouping Options button**. The Grouping Intervals dialog box will open.

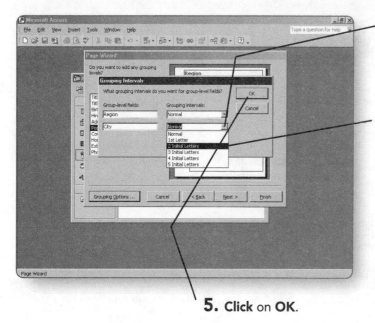

2. **Click** on the **down arrow** to the right of the Grouping intervals list box. A menu will appear.

3. **Click** on the **interval** you want. The interval will appear in the list box.

4. **Repeat Steps 2** and **3** until you set all grouping intervals.

5. **Click** on **OK**.

> ### NOTE
> Grouping intervals are available only for fields on which you've already specified a grouping level.

Specifying a Sort Order

Using the Page Wizard, you can sort up to four different fields in either ascending (the default) or descending order.

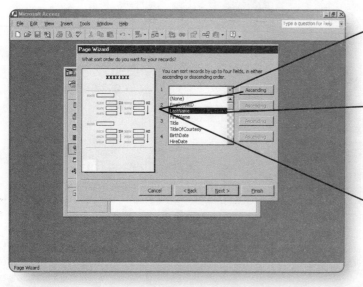

1. **Click** on the **down arrow** to the right of the first field. A menu will appear.

2. **Click** on the **first field** on which you want to sort your page. The ascending sort order will be automatically applied.

3. **Click** on the **Ascending button** to change the sort order to descending, if desired.

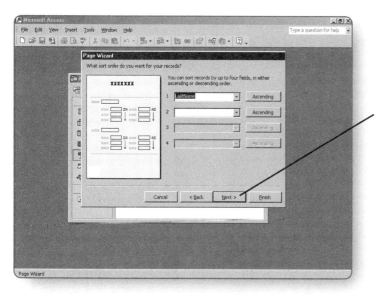

4. **Repeat Steps 1, 2,** and **3** until you select all sort orders.

5. **Click** on **Next** to continue.

Finishing the Page

In the final step of the Page Wizard, you'll create a page title and select the view you want to use when opening the page for the first time.

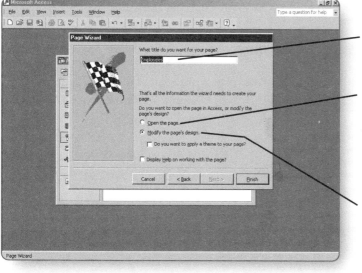

1. **Enter** a **name** for your page in the text box.

2a. **Click** on the **Open the page option button** to open the page in Page view.

OR

2b. **Click** on the **Modify the page's design option button** to open the page in Design view.

3. Click on the **Do you want to apply a theme to your page check box** if you want to open the Theme dialog box when you finish your page. You can apply a design theme, similar to a style, in this dialog box.

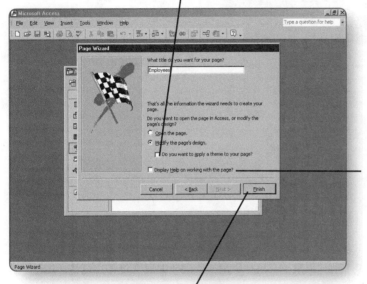

CAUTION

You must choose the Modify the page's design option (Step 2b rather than 2a) if you want to apply a theme.

---

4. Click on the **Display Help on working with the page check box** if you want to display a help window when you open the page.

5. Click on **Finish**. The page will save as an HTML file and will open based on your instructions in Step 2.

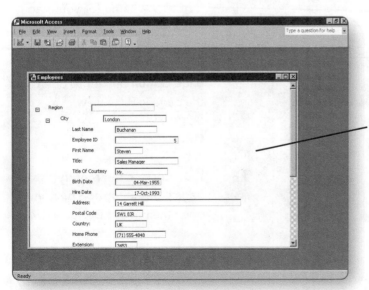

Or, if you chose to add a theme, the Theme dialog box will appear. See the following section, "Adding a Theme," for help with it.

If you open your page in Page view, you'll see exactly how it will look on the Web.

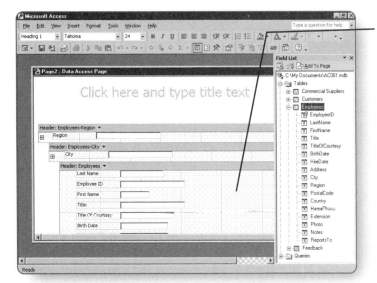

If you choose the option to modify the page's design, it will open in Design view. Design view includes space for you to enter a title and body text. Click on the areas that prompt you with "Click here and type title text" and "Click here and type body text" and then enter the desired text.

TIP

If you decide you want to start over again after creating a page, you can delete it by selecting it in the main database window and pressing the Delete key.

Adding a Theme

If you click the Do you want to apply a theme to your page check box on the final step of the Page Wizard, the Theme dialog box will open before displaying your page in Design view. A *theme* is similar to a report or form style and includes a group of headings, bullets, and hyperlinks that blend together.

TIP

You can also open the Theme dialog box and choose a theme at any time from Design view by choosing Format, Theme.

1. Click on the **theme** you want to apply from the Choose a Theme list. A sample of the theme will display on the right side of the dialog box.

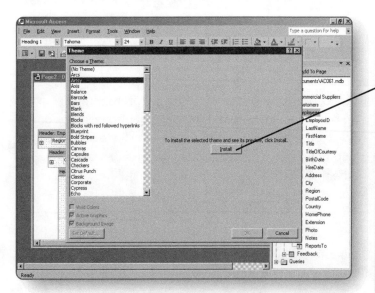

CAUTION

Not all themes are available upon initial installation. If you choose a theme that isn't installed yet, the preview box will display an Install button that you can click on to install the selected theme. You must have the Office or Access CD in your CD-ROM drive to complete this installation.

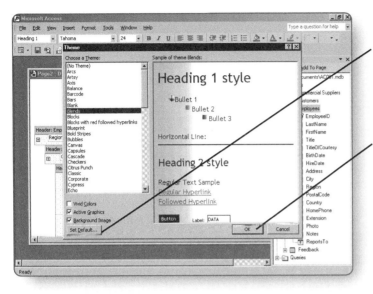

2. (Optional) **Click** on the **Set Default button** to set the selected theme as your default theme for all future pages.

3. Click on **OK**. The data access page will open in Design view.

Previewing Your Data Access Page

You can preview what your data access page will look like on the Web from either Page view or Design view.

1. Click on **File**. The File menu will appear.

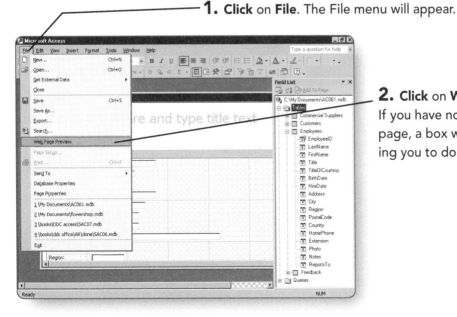

2. Click on **Web Page Preview**. If you have not yet saved your page, a box will appear prompting you to do so.

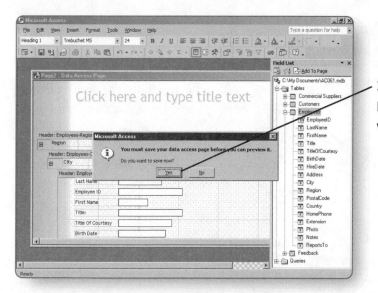

3. Click on **Yes**. The Save As Data Access Page dialog box will open.

4. Type a **name** for the page. The default name is the name of the table or query from which the data comes.

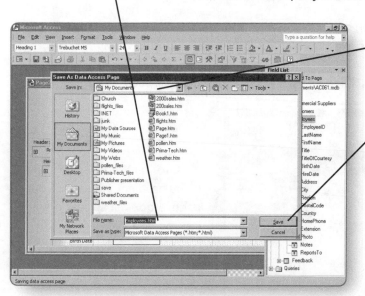

5. Change the **save location** if needed. You can save to your local hard disk or to a Web or FTP location.

6. Click on **Save**. The page will be saved.

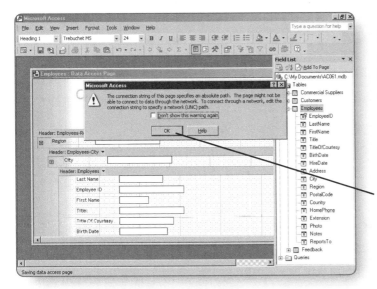

If you chose a location on your hard disk to save to rather than an Internet location, a warning box will appear about using an absolute path. An *absolute path* points to a specific location rather than a location in relation to the referring page.

7. Click on **OK**. The warning box will close.

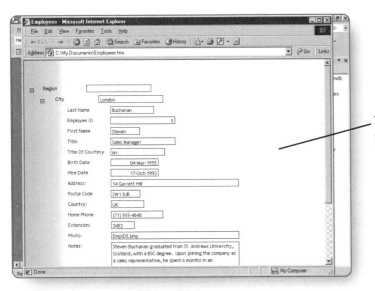

The data access page will open in Internet Explorer.

Part VII Review Questions

1. What data type should you set in Table Design view for a field that you want to function as a hyperlink? *See "Adding Hyperlinks to a Table in Design View" in Chapter 26*

2. What command do you use to insert a hyperlink column in Datasheet view? *See "Adding Hyperlink Columns in Datasheet View" in Chapter 26*

3. When typing data into a hyperlink type field, do you need to do anything special to make the entered text appear underlined? *See "Entering Hyperlinks in Tables" in Chapter 26*

4. What happens when you click on a hyperlink that points to an e-mail address? *See "Testing Your Hyperlink" in Chapter 26*

5. On a form, how can you place a hyperlink that is not associated with any particular field in a table? *See "Adding a Hyperlink Label to a Form" in Chapter 26*

6. What is a data access page, and why might you want to use one? *See "Understanding Data Access Pages" in Chapter 27*

7. What choices about layout can you make when creating a Columnar AutoPage? *See "Creating a Columnar AutoPage" in Chapter 27*

8. What options can you choose for your data access page with the Page Wizard? *See "Creating a Page with the Page Wizard" in Chapter 27*

9. What's the difference between grouping priority and grouping interval? *See "Changing the Grouping Priority" and "Setting Grouping Intervals" in Chapter 27*

10. When you preview your data access page, what program does it open in? *See "Previewing Your Data Access Page" in Chapter 27*

PART VIII

Appendixes

A

Installing Office XP

Access is part of the Office XP suite. Installing Office really is quick and painless—place the CD in your computer's CD-ROM drive and follow the wizard's instructions. In this appendix, you'll learn how to:

- Install Office on your computer
- Add or remove Office components
- Repair or reinstall Office

Installing the Software

You might have purchased Access separately or as part of the Office XP suite of programs. Either way, the installation process is similar. This appendix shows the Office XP installation process.

1. Insert the **Office XP CD-ROM** into your computer's CD-ROM drive. The Setup program will start, and the Microsoft Office Setup dialog box will open.

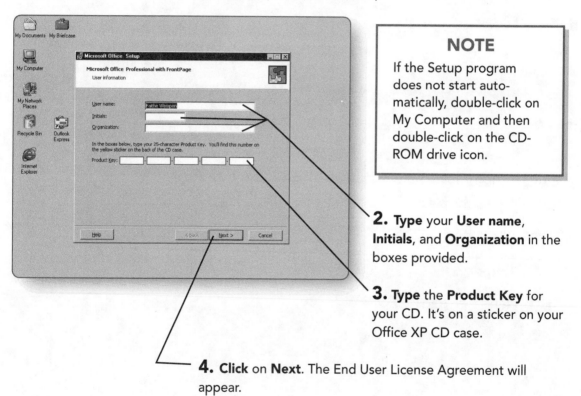

NOTE

If the Setup program does not start automatically, double-click on My Computer and then double-click on the CD-ROM drive icon.

2. Type your **User name**, **Initials**, and **Organization** in the boxes provided.

3. Type the **Product Key** for your CD. It's on a sticker on your Office XP CD case.

4. Click on **Next**. The End User License Agreement will appear.

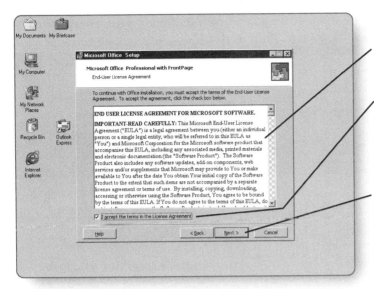

5. **Read** the **License Agreement**.

6. **Click** on the **I accept the terms in the License Agreement option button**. The option will be selected.

7. **Click** on **Next**. The installation type controls will appear.

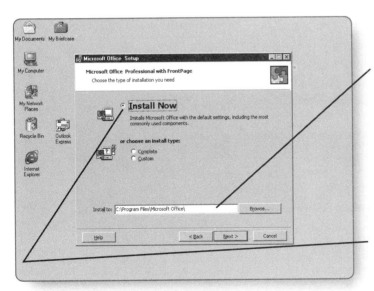

8. (Optional) **Change** the **installation path** in the Install to box if needed.

In most cases, the default path is fine, but you might need to change it if you don't have enough room on your C drive.

9a. **Click** on the **Install Now button**. Use this option to install Office on your computer with the default settings. This is the recommended installation for most users.

OR

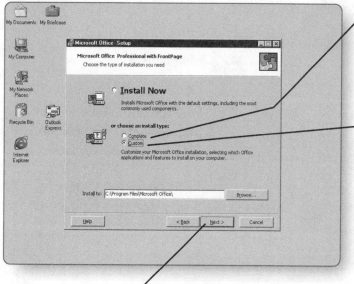

9b. Click on the **Complete button** if you want to install every available component.

OR

9c. Click on the **Custom button** if you want to choose which components to install or where to install them. The installation location options will appear. Then see the next section, "Choosing Components," for guidance.

10. Click on **Next** to continue. A confirmation screen will appear.

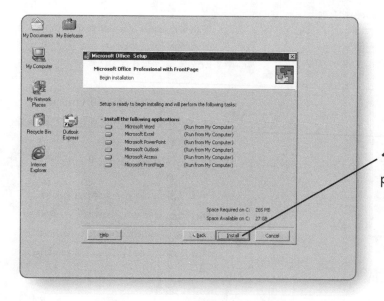

11. Click on **Install**. The Setup program will begin copying files.

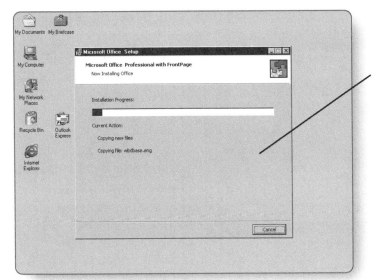

12. Wait while the **Office software** installs on your computer. A confirmation message will appear when it's done.

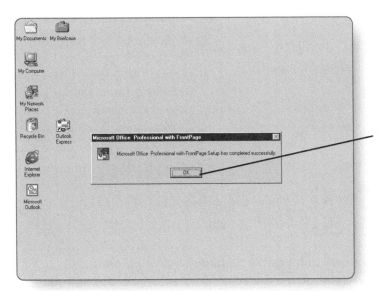

13. Click on **OK** to accept the confirmation.

Choosing Components

If you selected option 9c in the previous section, you have the choice of installing the different programs and components in Office XP.

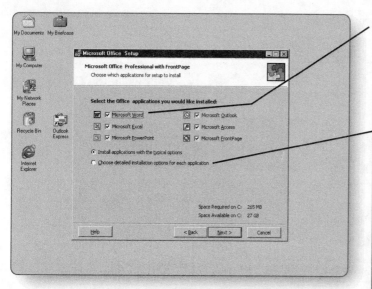

1. Click on the **check boxes** to deselect the programs that you don't want to install.

2. Go to **Step 10** of the preceding procedure.

Working with Maintenance Mode

Maintenance Mode is a feature of the Setup program. Whenever you run the Setup program again, after the initial installation, Maintenance Mode starts automatically. It enables you to add or remove features, repair your Office installation (for example, if files have become corrupted), and remove Office completely. There are several ways to rerun the Setup program (and thus enter Maintenance Mode):

- Reinsert the Office CD (or Access CD). The Setup program might start automatically.

- If the Setup program does not start automatically, double-click on the CD icon in the My Computer window. This will either start the Setup program or open a list of files. If it opens a list of files, double-click on Setup.exe.

- From the Control Panel in Windows, click on the Add/Remove Programs button. Then, on the Install/Uninstall tab, click on Microsoft Office (or Microsoft Access) in the list and, finally, click on the Add/Remove button.

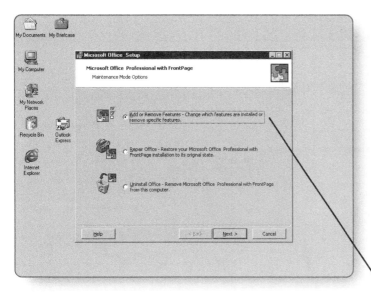

After entering Maintenance Mode, choose the button for the activity you want. Each option is briefly described in the following sections.

Adding and Removing Components

You can specify which components you want to install or uninstall.

1. Click on the **Add or Remove Features button** in Maintenance Mode. The Features to install window will appear.

NOTE

Some features will attempt to automatically install themselves as you are working. If you have set a feature to be installed on first use, attempt to access that feature. You will be prompted to insert your Office XP CD, and the feature will be installed without further prompting.

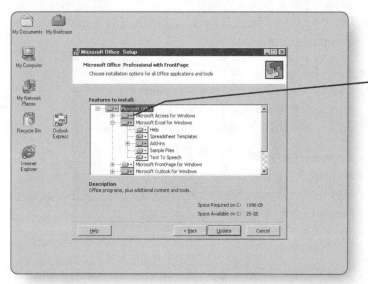

2. Click on **a plus sign (+)** to expand a list of features for a program or category. The features under it will appear.

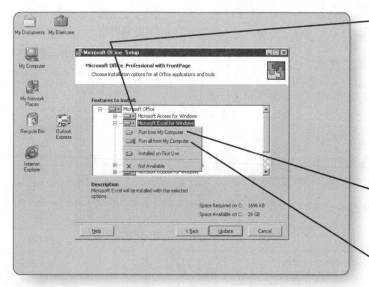

3. Click on the **down arrow** to the right of the hard drive icon for a feature. A menu of available options for the feature will appear.

4. Click on the **setting** you want for that feature:

- **Run from My Computer**. The component will be fully installed.

- **Run all from My Computer**. The component and all subcomponents beneath it will be fully installed.

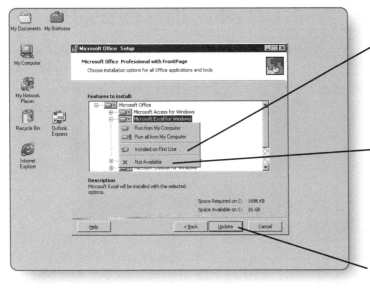

- **Installed on First Use**. The first time you try to access the component, you will be prompted to insert the Office CD to install it.

- **Not Available**. The component will not be installed.

5. **Repeat Steps 2 through 4** as needed.

6. Click on **Update**. The needed files will be copied or removed.

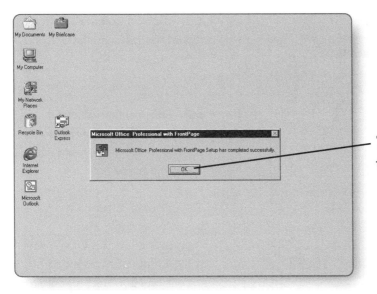

7. Click on **OK** when prompted that the setup is complete.

Repairing or Reinstalling Office

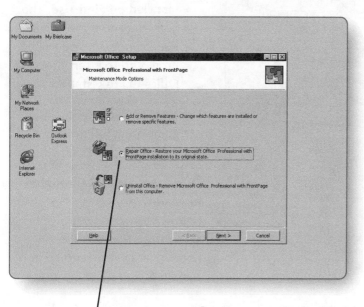

If an Office program is behaving strangely or refuses to work, chances are good that a needed file has become corrupted. But which file? You have no way of knowing, so you can't fix the problem yourself.

If this happens, you can either repair Office or completely reinstall it. Both options are accessed from the Repair Office button in Maintenance Mode.

1. Click on the **Repair Office button** in Maintenance Mode.

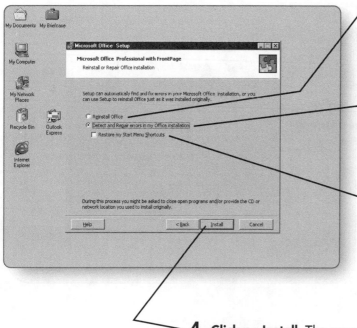

2a. Click on **Reinstall Office** to repeat the last installation.

OR

2b. Click on Detect and Repair errors in my Office installation to simply fix what's already in place.

3. (Optional) **Click** on the **Restore my Start Menu Shortcuts check box** if some of the Office programs do not appear on your Start menu even though they are installed.

4. Click on **Install**. The process will start.

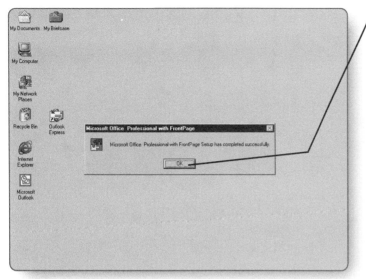

5. Click on **OK** to accept the confirmation that setup has completed successfully.

> **TIP**
>
> You can also repair individual Office programs by opening the Help menu in each program and clicking on Detect and Repair. This works well if you are sure that one certain program is causing the problem, and it's quicker than asking the Setup program to check all the installed programs.

Removing Office from Your PC

In the unlikely event that you should need to remove Office from your PC completely, click on Remove Office from the maintenance mode screen. Then follow the prompts to remove it from your system.

After removing Office, you will probably have a few remnants left behind that the Uninstall routine didn't catch. For example, there will probably still be a Microsoft Office folder in your Program Files folder or wherever you installed the program. You can delete that folder yourself.

> **CAUTION**
>
> If you plan to reinstall Office later and you have created any custom templates, toolbars, or other items, you might want to leave the Microsoft Office folder alone so that those items will be available to you after you reinstall.

B

Office Program Basics

If you have not worked with other Office XP programs, this appendix can help you become familiar with some of the standard program features. In this appendix, you'll learn how to:

- Use menus
- Use toolbars
- Work with dialog boxes
- Use the Help system
- Use task panes
- Browse for file locations

Using Menus

You need to issue commands in order to use Access. Menus are one of the most common ways to issue commands and navigate in Access.

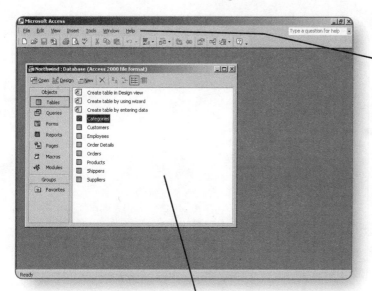

The menu bar, directly below the Access title bar, includes several menu option names that open groups of menu commands. Depending on where you are in Access and what you're doing, the menu structure will change, providing appropriate menu options.

NOTE

The illustrations in this appendix show an open database because some of the menus and dialog boxes shown are not available unless a database is open. You learn how to open a database in Chapter 4, "Creating a Table with the Table Wizard." The database shown here is the Northwind database, a sample that comes with Access.

Opening a Menu

1. Click on **File**. A menu of available commands will appear.

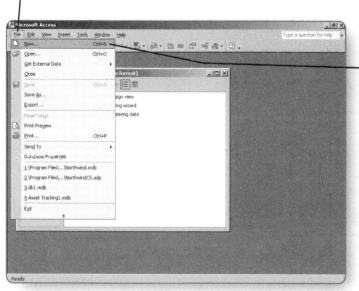

2. Click on the **menu command** you want to perform, such as New.

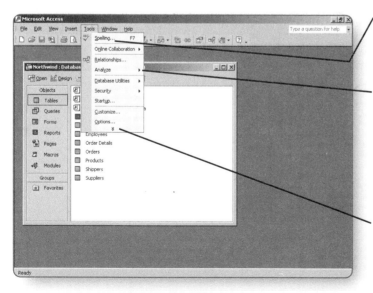

When you click on a menu command that is followed by an ellipsis, a dialog box will open.

When you click on a menu command that is followed by a right arrow, another menu will appear. Then click on a command in that menu to perform the command.

Menus initially display only the most commonly used menu commands. To view additional commands, click on the double down arrows at the bottom of a menu.

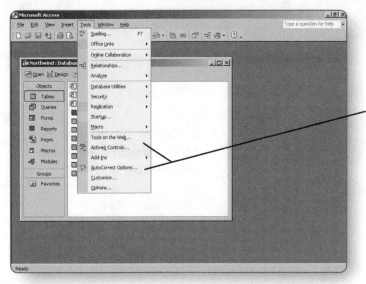

The menu then displays additional, hidden menu choices. Click on the one you need, and the next time you open the menu, it won't be hidden.

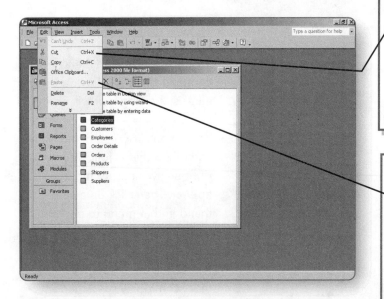

TIP

Many Access menu commands have shortcut keys. A shortcut key lets you bypass the menu by pressing a keyboard command such as Ctrl+X.

NOTE

Sometimes menu commands appear dimmed. This means they aren't available to use at this time. For example, the Save command on the File menu will appear dimmed if you haven't created new data.

Using a Shortcut Menu

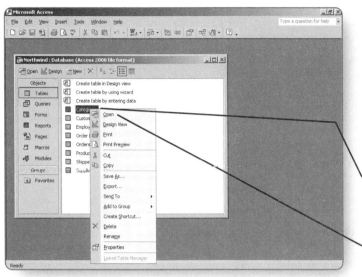

Access offers a special kind of menu called a *shortcut menu*. A shortcut menu displays the specific menu commands that apply to a particular item you select. For example, this item can be text, a graphics object, a row, or a column.

1. Right-click on the **item** whose shortcut menu you want to see. The menu will appear.

2. Click on the **menu command** to perform it.

Using Toolbars

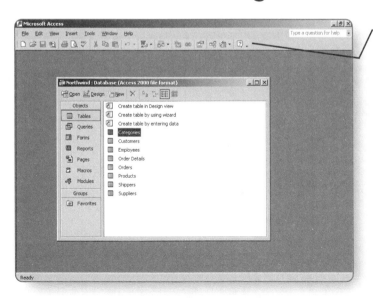

Toolbars make it easy to use the program's most common features and functions. If you use other Office XP applications, such as Word or Excel, some of these toolbars and buttons may look familiar; there are many similarities among the Office XP products. When you click on a button on the toolbar, you either perform a command or open a dialog box. Some of the buttons on the toolbar change depending on which window is active.

As with menus, not all buttons are available at all times; unavailable buttons appear dimmed.

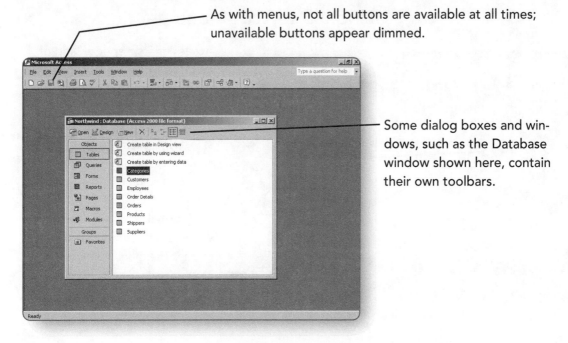

Some dialog boxes and windows, such as the Database window shown here, contain their own toolbars.

Finding Out What a Toolbar Button Does

You can use the Access ScreenTips feature to find out what a particular toolbar button does.

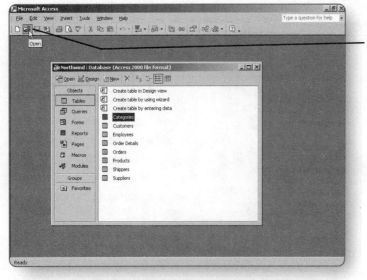

Hover the mouse over the button without clicking on it. A ScreenTip will appear describing what the button does.

Using Toolbar Buttons That Display Menus

Some toolbar buttons, such as the Office Links or New Object buttons on the Standard toolbar, include a down arrow to the right of the button that opens a menu.

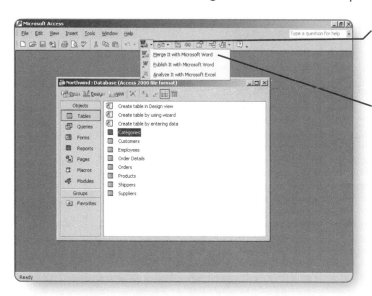

1. Click on the **down arrow** next to the toolbar button. A menu will appear.

2. From this menu, **click** on a **command** to perform it.

Working with Dialog Boxes

You'll use dialog boxes frequently in Access to make choices, issue commands, and apply formatting.

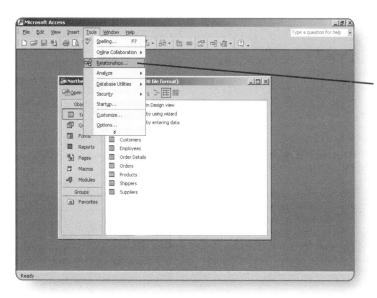

When you click on a menu command followed by an ellipsis, a dialog box opens. The name of the dialog box appears in the title bar.

Dialog boxes can contain any of the following elements:

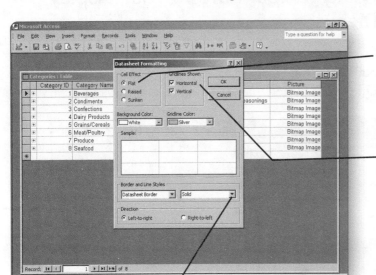

- **Option button**. Click on the option button to select that option. You can select only one option in a group of option buttons.

- **Check box**. Click to put a check mark in a check box, thereby selecting that option. You can select more than one check box in a group of check boxes.

- **List box**. Click on the down arrow next to the list box. A list of options will appear. In a long list, you can use the up and down arrows to scroll through the list box options.

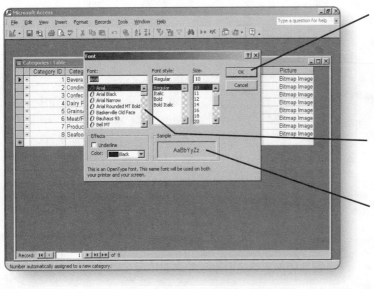

- **Command button**. Click on a command button to perform the command. A command button that includes an ellipsis will open a secondary dialog box.

- **Scroll box**. Drag within the scroll box to scroll the list up or down.

- **Preview area**. Look at the preview area to view how your choices will appear.

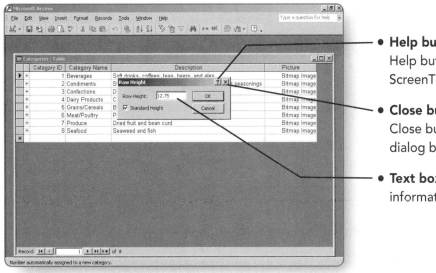

- **Help button**. Click on the Help button to activate ScreenTips help.

- **Close button**. Click on the Close button to close the dialog box.

- **Text box**. Enter data or information in a text box.

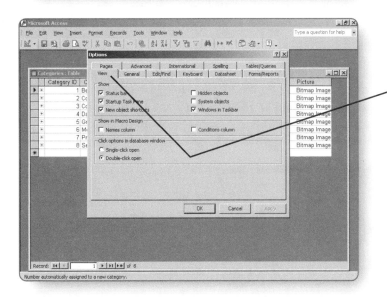

- **Tab**. Click on a Tab (for example, View) to move to another sheet in the dialog box.

Getting Help

Access provides several ways of getting help if you have a problem using the program. These help features include the Office Assistant, which enables you to ask questions and get answers; the Ask a Question box, which is a streamlined version of the Office Assistant; the Microsoft Access Help window, which includes a detailed help index; and the What's This? command, which enables you to point to an object or area and ask what it is.

Using the Office Assistant

The Office Assistant provides context-sensitive help and lets you ask questions about a task you want to perform.

TIP

Unlike in earlier versions of Access, the Office Assistant doesn't appear automatically when you start the program. To display the Office Assistant again, click on Help, Show the Office Assistant from the menu bar.

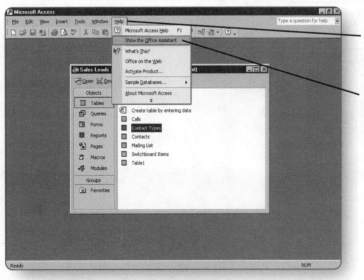

1. **Click** on **Help**. The Help menu will open.

2. **Click** on **Show the Office Assistant**. The Office Assistant will appear.

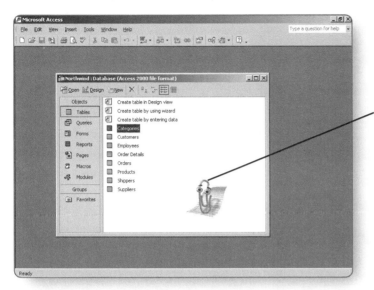

3. Click on the **Office Assistant**. The Office Assistant message balloon will appear.

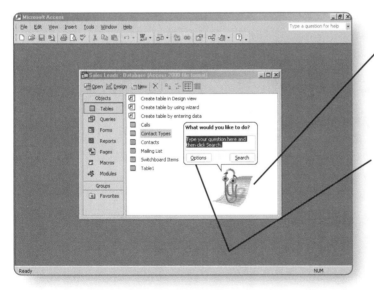

To change the icon, click on the Options button in the Office Assistant balloon. In the Office Assistant dialog box that opens, go to the Gallery tab to choose another Assistant icon such as The Dot, Merlin, Mother Nature, or Rocky.

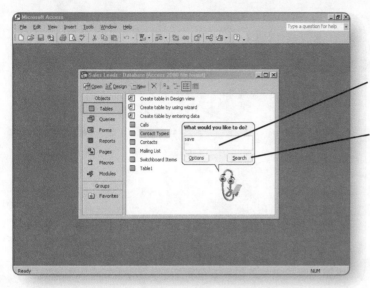

4. Enter a **specific question or keyword** in the text box.

5. Click on the **Search button** or press **Enter**. A new topic list will appear that relates to this question.

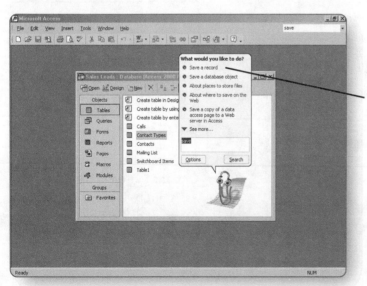

6. Click on the **topic** that you want to see.

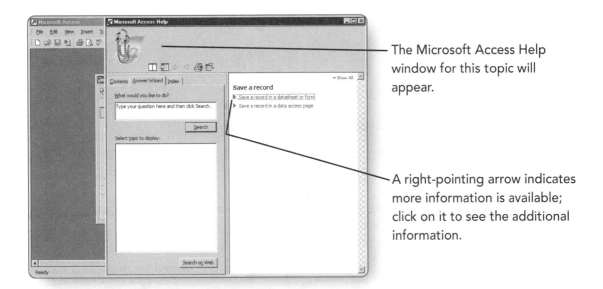

The Microsoft Access Help window for this topic will appear.

A right-pointing arrow indicates more information is available; click on it to see the additional information.

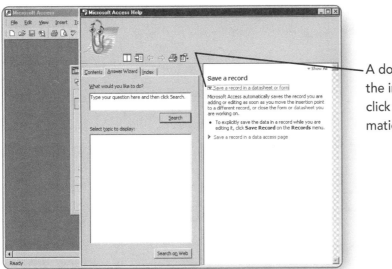

A down-pointing arrow indicates the information is collapsible; click here to hide the information below it.

Using the Ask a Question Feature

If you don't want to go to the trouble of turning on the Office Assistant or just plain don't like dealing with cartoon characters, try the Ask a Question box, a new feature in Office XP programs.

1. Click in the **Ask a Question** box. The insertion point will appear there.

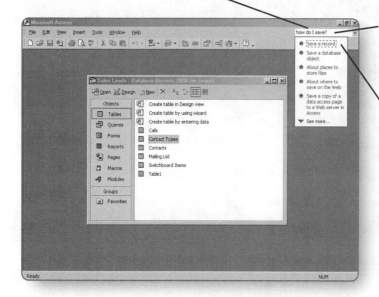

2. Type your **question** or a **keyword** about which you want information.

3. Press Enter. A drop-down list will appear. This list contains the same options as the Office Assistant results from the preceding section.

4. Click on the **topic** you want to see. The Microsoft Access Help window will appear.

Using the Microsoft Access Help Index

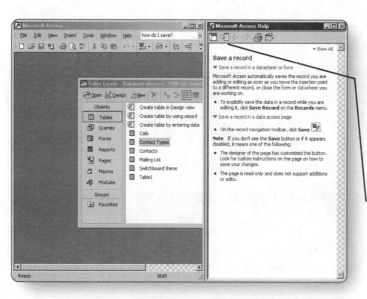

You can also search the Microsoft Access Help index for the exact term or topic for which you're seeking help. This process starts from inside the Microsoft Access Help window, so use one of the preceding procedures to access it. Then do the following.

1. Click on the **Show button** if the navigation pane does not already appear. A pane with three tabs will appear.

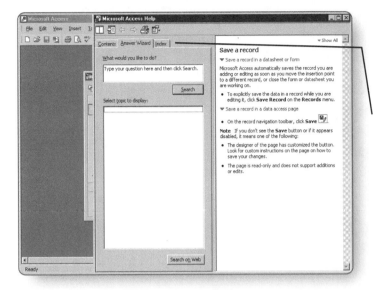

2. Click on the **Index tab**. A complete help index will appear.

3a. Enter the **topic** you want to search for in the Type keywords text box. The index will move to this entry.

OR

3b. Click on a **keyword** from the Or choose keywords list.

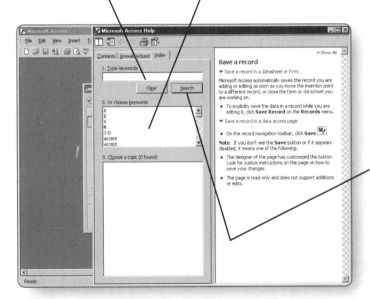

4. Click on the **Search button**. The Choose a topic list will display potential matching index entries.

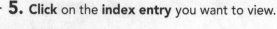

5. Click on the **index entry** you want to view.

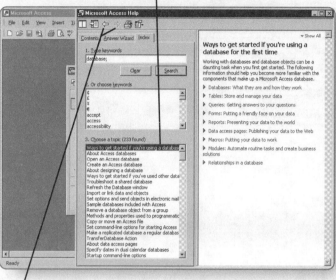

The help topic will appear on the right side of the window.

TIP

Click on the Back button to go back to a previously viewed topic. You can then use the Forward button to go forward again after going backward.

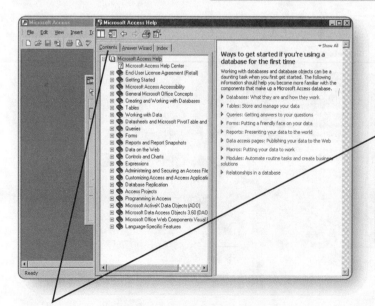

TIP

To see a list of help topics by category, click on the Contents tab. A table of contents listing the help topics by category will display.

Printing a Help Topic

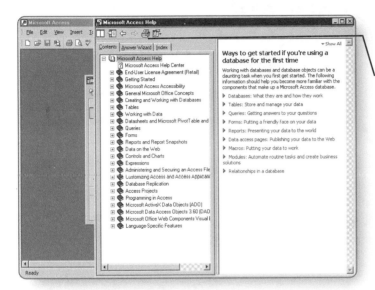

Click on the Print button in the Microsoft Access Help window to print the current help topic on your default printer. Be sure your printer is turned on before clicking this button.

Exiting Help

After you find the help information you need, you can exit the help system and return to Access.

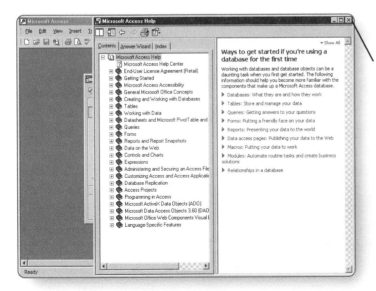

Click on the Close button to exit Microsoft Access Help.

Hiding the Office Assistant

Sometimes the Office Assistant just seems to get in the way on the Access desktop. You can hide it from view until the next time you need it.

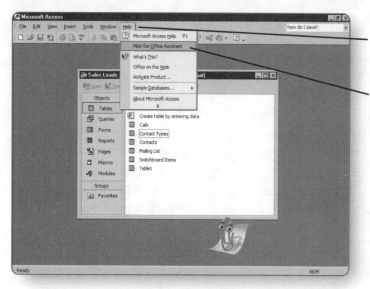

1. **Click** on **Help**. The Help menu will open.

2. **Click** on **Hide the Office Assistant**. The Office Assistant will be hidden from view.

TIP

You can also right-click on the Assistant and choose Hide from the shortcut menu that displays.

Redisplaying the Office Assistant

To display the Assistant again, repeat the same basic procedure as for hiding it, but choose Show the Office Assistant.

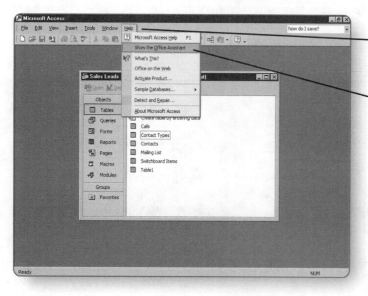

1. **Click** on **Help**. The Help menu will open.

2. **Click** on **Show the Office Assistant**. The Office Assistant will reappear.

Using What's This? to Get Help

Access includes a feature called What's This? Using this feature, you can access a ScreenTip for a menu command, toolbar button, or other item on the screen.

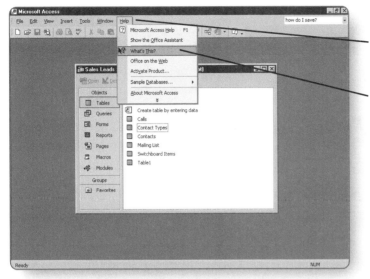

1. **Click** on **Help**. The Help menu will appear.

2. **Click** on **What's This?** What's This? will be activated.

3. **Click** on the **toolbar button, menu command**, or **part of the screen** with which you want help.

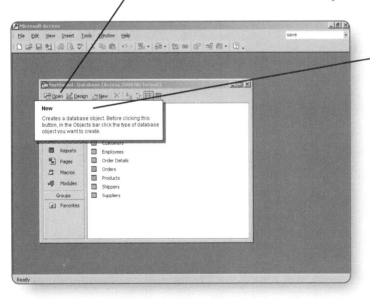

A ScreenTip will appear providing basic information about the item you selected.

Using What's This? in a Dialog Box

You can also access What's This? from a dialog box, but the steps are a little different.

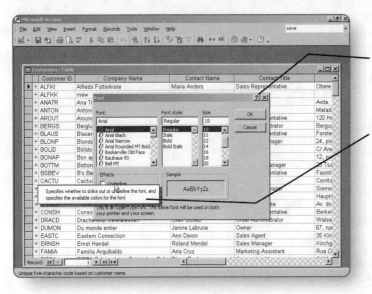

1. Click on the **? button** in the upper-right corner of the dialog box to activate What's This?

2. Click on the **part** of the **dialog box** with which you need help. The ScreenTip will appear.

Using the Task Pane

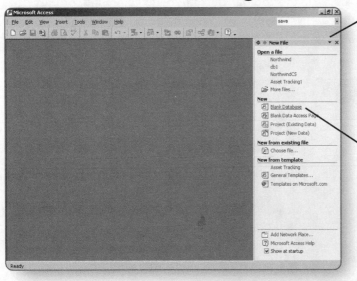

The task pane is a new feature in Office XP programs. It appears at the right side of the program window and offers shortcuts to common commands.

1. Click on a **shortcut** in the task pane. The command associated with that shortcut will execute.

NOTE

In Access, the task pane appears by default only when no database is open. That's why you did not see it in the illustrations earlier in this appendix. If the task pane does not appear, choose View, Toolbars, Task Pane. Choosing File, New will also display it.

Switching among Task Panes

Depending on what you are doing, different task panes might be available.

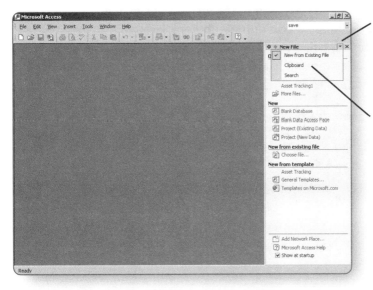

1. **Click** on the **down-pointing arrow** in the upper-right corner of the task pane. A menu of available task panes will appear.

2. **Click** on the **task pane** that you want to see. The selected task pane will appear.

For example, you can display the Clipboard as a task pane.

Browsing for File Locations

Access, like all Office XP programs, stores your work in files. When you save a file, you can store it in the default save location (C:\My Documents), or you can change the location to a different drive or folder before saving. Similarly, when opening a file, you can choose from the files in the default location (again, C:\My Documents), or you can browse other locations to find the file you want to open.

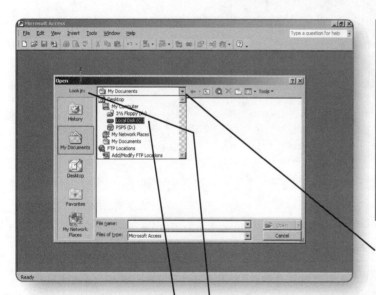

NOTE

The following steps show the Open dialog box as an example, but the procedure is the same for opening and saving, as well as for any other procedures that require you to locate and specify a file.

1. Click on the **down arrow** to open a list of locations.

NOTE

In the Save As dialog box, this list is called Save in; in the Open dialog box, it's called Look in.

2. Click on the **drive** you want. Icons for each of the folders on that drive will appear.

3. Double-click on the **folder** you want.

NOTE

Depending on where you want to save, you might need to move through several levels of folders to arrive at the one you want.

4. Continue saving or **opening** normally.

Other Ways to Navigate Folder Listings

Besides the basic method shown in the preceding steps, there are other ways to move around your drives and folders when saving or opening files.

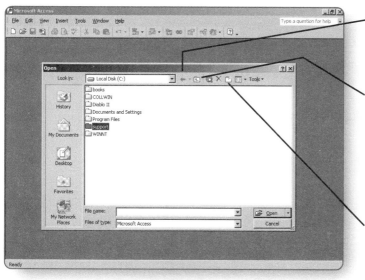

Click on the Back button to go back to the previously viewed location.

Click on the Up One Level button to move up one level in the folder hierarchy. For example, if you are viewing C:\Test\ Data and you click Up One Level, you go to C:\Test.

Click on the Create New Folder button to create a new folder on the fly.

In all Office XP programs, the Save and Open dialog boxes include a Places bar at the left side of the dialog box. The Places bar contains the following shortcuts.

Click on the History button to see a list of recently used data files from which you can choose.

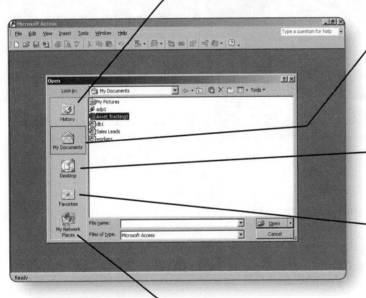

Click on the My Documents button to return to the My Documents folder.

Click on the Desktop button to display the folder corresponding to your Windows desktop.

Click on the Favorites button to display the list of Favorites you have saved in Internet Explorer.

Click on the My Network Places button to browse your local area network for file locations. (Depending on your version of Windows, this button might be replaced by a Web Folders button.)

Using Keyboard Shortcuts

Access X includes numerous keyboard shortcuts listed on the right side of several of the menus; you may have even started using some of these. Access also has many other keyboard shortcuts, which help make using the software even easier and more convenient. Shortcuts enable you to execute commands without using the mouse to activate menus. In this appendix, you'll learn how to:

- Get up to speed with frequently used keyboard shortcuts
- Use keyboard combinations to edit text and data

General Shortcuts

Access includes many common shortcuts that you can use in several parts of the program, such as in the Database Window, Datasheet view, Form view, and so on. The following table lists a number of these general shortcuts.

TIP

Most Windows applications share the same keyboard combinations to execute common commands. Once you get accustomed to using some of these keyboard shortcuts in Access, try them out on some of the other Microsoft Office programs.

To Execute This Command	Do This
Display the Office Assistant	Press F1
Create a new database	Press Ctrl+N
Open an existing database	Press Ctrl+O
Save the current object	Press Ctrl+S
Open the Save As dialog box	Press F12
Print the selected object	Press Ctrl+P
Undo the previous action	Press Ctrl+Z

Datasheet View Shortcuts

You can use shortcut keys to easily navigate in Datasheet view, as illustrated in this table.

To Execute This Command	Do This
Go to the next field	Press Tab or right arrow
Go to the last field in the current record	Press End
Return to the previous field	Press Shift+Tab or the left arrow
Go to the first field in the current record	Press Home
Go to the next record	Press the down arrow
Go to the last record	Press Ctrl+down arrow
Go to the last field in the last record	Press Ctrl+End
Return to the previous record	Press the up arrow
Return to the current field in the first record	Press Ctrl+up arrow
Return to the first field in the first record	Press Ctrl+Home
Move down one screen	Press Page Down
Move up one screen	Press Page Up
Move one screen right	Press Ctrl+Page Down
Move one screen left	Press Ctrl+Page Up
Go to the record number box	Press F5

Form View Shortcuts

When you're in Form view, you can use a variety of different shortcuts, many of which are similar to the ones you use in Datasheet view. This table lists the most common shortcuts.

To Execute This Command	Do This
Go to the next field	Press Tab
Return to the previous field	Press Shift+Tab
Go to the last field in the current record	Press End
Go to the first field in the current record	Press Home
Go to the next record	Press Ctrl+Page Down
Return to the previous record	Press Ctrl+Page Up
Go to the last field in the last record	Press Ctrl+End
Return to the first field in the first record	Press Ctrl+Home
Move down one page	Press Page Down
Move up one page	Press Page Up
Go to the record number box	Press F5

Print Preview Shortcuts

Print Preview also has similar shortcuts. These include the shortcuts listed in the following table.

To Execute This Command	Do This
Open the Print dialog box	Press P or Ctrl+P
Open the Page Setup dialog box	Press S
Zoom in and out of the page	Press Z
Cancel Print Preview	Press C or Esc
Scroll down in small increments	Press the down arrow
Scroll up in small increments	Press the up arrow
Scroll to the right in small increments	Press the right arrow
Scroll to the left in small increments	Press the left arrow
Scroll down one full screen	Press Page Down
Scroll up one full screen	Press Page Up
Go to the bottom of the page	Press Ctrl+down arrow
Go to the top of the page	Press Ctrl+up arrow
Go to the right edge of the page	Press End or Ctrl+right arrow
Go to the left edge of the page	Press Home or Ctrl+left arrow
Go to the lower-right corner of the page	Press Ctrl+End
Go to the upper-left corner of the page	Press Ctrl+Home
Go to the page number box	Press F5

Text and Data Shortcuts

When you need to enter and edit extensive amounts of data, such as in tables or forms, you'll be glad to use as many shortcuts as possible.

Selection Shortcuts

Before you can edit the text in your Access tables, forms, and reports, you'll need to select it. This table shows you how to use keyboard combinations to select text.

To Execute This Command	Do This
Select the character to the right of the cursor	Press Shift+right arrow
Select the character to the left of the cursor	Press Shift+left arrow
Select the entire word to the right of the cursor	Press Ctrl+Shift+right arrow
Select the entire word to the left of the cursor	Press Ctrl+Shift+left arrow
Select the next field	Press Tab

Editing Shortcuts

Once you select the text to which you want to make the editing changes, apply one of the combinations in the following table.

To Execute This Command	Do This
Delete the character to the left of the cursor	Press Backspace
Delete the character to the right of the cursor	Press Delete
Delete the word to the left of the cursor	Press Ctrl+Backspace
Delete the word to the right of the cursor	Press Ctrl+Delete
Cut the selected object/text	Press Ctrl+X
Copy the selected object/text	Press Ctrl+C
Paste the selected object/text	Press Ctrl+V
Delete the selected object/text	Press Delete
Rename the selected object/text	Press F2
Search for a word or words	Press Ctrl+F

To Execute This Command	Do This
Replace a word or words	Press Ctrl+H
Undo an edit	Press Ctrl+Z or Alt+Backspace
Undo changes in the current field or record	Press Esc
Check spelling	Press F7
Add a new record	Press Ctrl+plus sign (+)
Delete the current record	Press Ctrl+minus sign (-)
Save changes to the current record	Press Shift+Enter
Insert the same value from the previous record	Press Ctrl+apostrophe (')

Menu Command Shortcuts

Finally, you may also want to use shortcut keys to activate menu commands instead of using the mouse. Use the shortcuts in this table to access menus.

To Execute This Command	Do This
Activate the menu bar	Press F10
Display a shortcut menu	Press Shift+F10
Display the program menu	Press Alt+spacebar
Select the next menu command	Press the down arrow
Go back to the previous menu command	Press the up arrow
Select the next option on the menu bar	Press the right arrow
Go back to the previous option on the menu bar	Press the left arrow
Close the visible menu	Press Alt
Close a submenu	Press Esc

D

Creating Effective Databases

Anyone can cobble together a database, but it takes some smart planning to create a usable database that doesn't waste storage space or user effort. When creating a database for business use, you can't afford to learn by trial and error what constitutes good database structure. In this appendix, you will:

- Plan your database tables
- Learn about database normalization

Planning Your Tables

At the minimum, a database needs one table. However, many beginners make the mistake of trying to put too much information in one table. Access is a relational database program, so it's meant to handle many tables and create relationships among them.

For example, in a database that keeps track of inventory, you might have the following tables:

- Supplier contact information

- Inventory orders

- Inventory items

- Payment terms

- Supplier types

TIP

Plan your tables before you create your database, because changing a table's structure after it contains data is difficult and can result in having to reenter some of the data.

Another mistake is to assume that each table must look like a stand-alone report. For example, you don't have to repeat a supplier's contact information with every inventory product entry; you can simply create a relationship between the table that contains the items and the table that contains the suppliers. Then, if you ever want a report or form that contains the combined information, you can easily create it.

Normalizing a Database Structure

When a database suffers from redundancy, waste, or other poor design, experts say it's not *normalized*. There are normalization rules that govern how a relational database should store information in tables.

There are five normalization rules, but the last three are fairly complicated and used mostly by database professionals. As a beginner, you really only need to know the first two to avoid major design mistakes.

Rule 1: Avoid Repeated Information

Suppose that you want to keep contact information on your inventory suppliers, along with a record of each order you place. If you keep it all in one table, you need to repeat the supplier's full name, address, and phone number in each order record, as shown here.

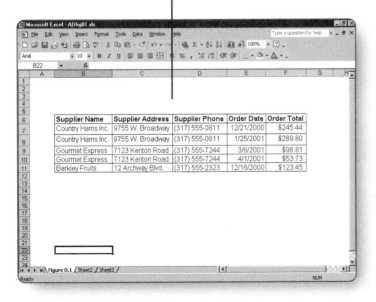

That's wasting space. And what if the supplier changes his address? You would have to change it in every order record for that supplier.

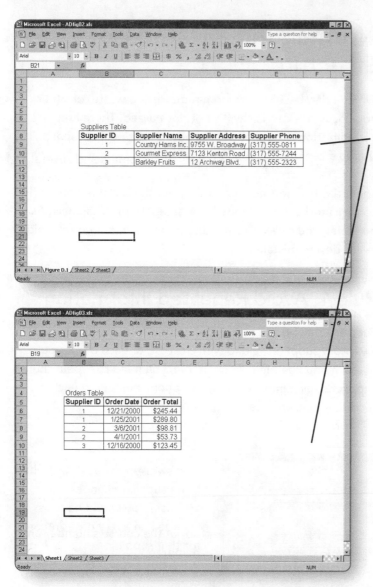

A better way is to assign each supplier an ID number. Then you include that ID number in two separate tables: one for the names and addresses and another for the orders.

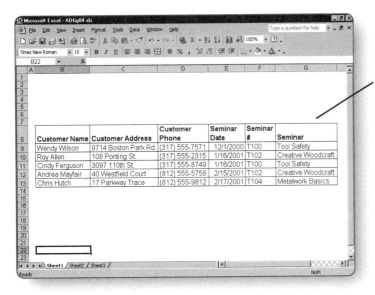

Rule 2: Avoid Redundant Data

Say that your company offers free seminars to customers about the benefits of your product lines. Your company has lots of customers and several different seminars. One way to keep track is to keep all the information in a single customer database.

But what if a customer wants to take more than one class? You would have to add a duplicate line in the table to list it, and then you have the problem described in Rule 1: multiple records with virtually identical entries.

Further, what if the only customer who has taken a certain class decides not to order from you anymore and needs to be removed from your customer database? When you delete that customer's record, you delete the information about the course's number and name, too.

The next three tables— Customers Table, Seminars Table, and Seminars Completed Table respectively—show a better way

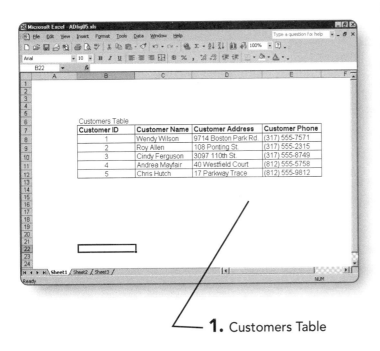

1. Customers Table

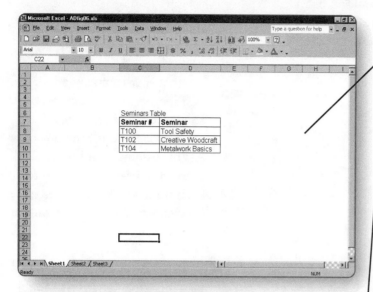

2. Seminars Table

3. Seminars Completed Table

More Table Design Tips

Good table organization boils down to a few principles:

- Each table should have one theme, such as Customer Contact Information or Orders Placed.

- If you see that you might end up repeating data in a table in the future plan now to split the information into its own table.

- To preserve a master list of information put it in its own table.

- Use ID numbers. They'll help you link tables later and avoid unnecessary typing errors.

- If you already have unique customer or employee numbers, you can use them; otherwise, use an Auto-Number field in Access to automatically generate a unique number for each record.

Glossary

Address. The URL of the Web site to which you want to link. An example of an address is http://www.microsoft.com. *See also Uniform Resource Locator.*

AutoForm. A basic automated form in either a columnar, tabular, or datasheet format.

AutoFormat. A way to automatically apply specific fonts, colors, and borders to a selected form or report. *See also Form and Report.*

AutoNumber. A data type that stores a unique incremented number for every record in a table. *See also Data type.*

AutoPage. A basic data access page created from an Access table or query.

AutoReport. A basic automated report in either a columnar or tabular format.

Browser. An external software program used to access and view World Wide Web pages. Microsoft Internet Explorer and Netscape Navigator are examples of browsers.

Chart wizard. A wizard that helps you create a report that contains a graphical representation of your data, either in summary or in detail.

Check box. A control that enables you to choose a particular option. A check mark in a check box indicates that an option is selected; no check mark indicates that the option is not selected. *See also Control.*

Click on. A way to perform an action by using the mouse to select a button, menu, or dialog box option.

Clipboard. A Windows holding area for transferring data.

Close button. A button you use to exit a dialog box, window, or Access itself.

Combo box. A control that contains a drop-down list from which you can select one of the listed values or you can enter a specific value not on the list.

Control. An object you place on a report or form. Text boxes, combo boxes, and option buttons are all examples of controls.

Criteria. Query and filter conditions that narrow the selected records or data. *See also Filter and Query.*

Current record. The unique selected record that you can use or modify.

Data access page. An Access form or report designed for the Web.

Data Entry mode. A mode that displays a blank table or form in which to enter data; temporarily hides all previously entered records from view.

Data type. A table field property that specifies the type of data you'll store in that field. Text, number, and date/time are examples of data types. *See also Field and Table.*

Database. A collection of information. In Access, objects such as forms, tables, reports, and queries make up a database.

Database window. A window that contains six tabs, each corresponding to one of the six objects that make up an Access database.

Database Wizard. A feature in Access that helps you create a new database complete with tables, reports, and forms by answering a few questions. *See also Wizard.*

Datasheet view. A view that displays table data in rows and columns, as in a spreadsheet. See *also View.*

Default. A value that automatically displays in a field or control.

Design grid. The bottom portion of the Select Query window in which you specify query criteria.

Design view. A view that allows you to design or modify the selected report, table, form, or query.

Detail query. A select query that contains all fields in all records. *See also Select query.*

Dialog box. A box that displays when you perform another action, such as clicking on a button or menu option. A dialog box either provides information or enables you to select additional options.

Display text. The text you want to display in a hyperlink field in a table.

Edit mode. A mode that enables you to enter data in a table or form; it also enables you to add records to the end of existing records.

Field. A column in a table. An individual field relates specifically to the record with which it intersects.

Filter. A specification that weeds out data you do not want, leaving only the data that meets a specific criterion or a set of criteria.

Filter by Form. A feature that lets you filter based on more than one criterion.

Filter by Selection. A feature that lets you select specific data in a table open in Datasheet view and then apply a basic filter.

Form. A database object you use to enter, view, and edit table data.

Form section. A way to divide a form; an Access form can have Detail, Form Header, Page Header, Page Footer, and Form Footer sections.

Form view. A view in which you can enter data into a form.

Hyperlink. In Access, a field data type that stores a link to a Web page or other object.

Hypertext Markup Language (HTML). A method of marking up or formatting documents for the World Wide Web.

Import. A method of transferring data from another source, such as a spreadsheet, into an Access table.

Internet. An international network of millions of computers.

Intranet. An internal corporate or organizational network that uses Internet technology.

Join lines. Lines in the Select Query window that relate data in one table to data in another.

Label. A control that displays descriptive text such as a title or caption.

Label wizard. A wizard that helps you create a report that contains labels organized in rows and columns for printing on peel-off sheets of labels.

Landscape. A page orientation that prints reports in a horizontal format.

List box. A control that contains a drop-down list from which you can select one of the listed values.

Menu. A command list that displays when you click on a menu name on the menu bar.

Menu bar. A horizontal bar located directly below the Access title bar that includes menu names.

Navigation buttons. Buttons that display in Datasheet and Form views that let you move to the first, last, next, and preceding records.

Office Assistant. A help feature that answers users' questions.

Option button. A small button that precedes a text option on an Access form; part of an option group. Sometimes referred to as a radio button.

Option group. A control that enables you to choose one of several displayed options, preceded by option buttons, check boxes, or toggle buttons.

Page view. A view in Access that displays a data access page as it will appear on the Internet.

PivotChart. Like a PivotTable, but in graphical chart format rather than a table. *See also PivotTable.*

PivotTable. A table that summarizes data from two or more fields, such as summarizing sales for each salesperson or each region based on orders entered.

Portrait. A page orientation that prints reports in a vertical format.

Primary key. One or more table fields that serve as a unique tag for each table record; this unique key relates the records in the current table to records in other tables.

Print Preview. A view that displays a report as it will look when you print it.

Query. A database object that extracts specific information from a database; it can also perform an action on this data.

Record. A row in a table.

Report. A database object that presents or analyzes database information in a printed format.

Report section. A way to divide a report; an Access report can have Detail, Report Header, Page Header, Page Footer, Report Footer, Group Header, and Group Footer sections.

ScreenTip. A tip that appears when you position the mouse pointer over a toolbar button or particular part of the screen.

Select query. A query that selects specific information from a database.

Simple Query Wizard. A wizard that helps you create a query by selecting fields from one or more tables or existing queries.

Sort. A command that organizes selected data in either ascending or descending order.

Style. A method of formatting objects using the same fonts, backgrounds, and colors.

Subaddress. The exact location in a Web page or document to which you want to link.

Subdatasheet. A datasheet within a datasheet that displays related table data for each individual record.

Summary query. A select query that summarizes information.

Table. A database object that serves as a collector of information about a related subject, organized by fields and records.

Table Wizard. A wizard that helps you create a new table by selecting fields from one or more sample tables.

Task pane. A window along the right side of the screen that provides access to file management tools, the Clipboard, and other objects.

Text box. A control that you place on a form or report to display table or query data.

Theme. A theme is similar to a report or form style and includes a group of headings, bullets, and hyperlinks that blend together.

Title bar. A horizontal bar located directly above the menu bar that displays the name of the open window.

Toolbar. A horizontal bar located below the menu bar that includes toolbar buttons that you click on to perform a specific action.

Toolbox. A toolbar that contains a series of buttons you use to create form or report controls.

Uniform Resource Locator (URL). The address of the Internet document, Web page, or object to which you want to link. An example of a URL is http://www.microsoft.com.

View. A window that lets you use an Access object in a particular way.

Wizard. An automated feature that guides you step-by-step through a process. In Access, you can use wizards to create databases, tables, reports, forms, and queries, for example.

World Wide Web. A graphical Internet environment accessed with a browser and organized with Web sites comprised of text, graphics, sound, and video.

Zoom. A way to reduce or enlarge the area you view in Print Preview.

Index

PRIMA TECH's *fast&easy* series

Fast Facts, Easy Access

Offering extraordinary value at a bargain price, the *fast & easy* series is dedicated to one idea: To help readers accomplish tasks as quickly and easily as possible. The unique visual teaching method combines concise tutorials and hundreds of screen shots to dramatically increase learning speed and retention of the material. With PRIMA TECH's *fast & easy* series, you simply look and learn.

Family Tree Maker® Version 8 Fast & Easy®: The Official Guide
0-7615-2998-5
U.S. $18.99 • Can. $28.95 • U.K. £13.99

Microsoft® Windows® Millennium Edition Fast & Easy®
0-7615-2739-7
U.S. $18.99 • Can. $28.95 • U.K. £13.99

Paint Shop Pro™ 7 Fast & Easy®
0-7615-3241-2
U.S. $18.99 • Can. $28.95 • U.K. £13.99

Quicken® 2001 Fast & Easy®
0-7615-2908-X
U.S. $18.99 • Can. $28.95 • U.K. £13.99

Microsoft® Works Suite 2001 Fast & Easy®
0-7615-3371-0
U.S. $24.99 • Can. $37.95 • U.K. £18.99

Microsoft® Access 2002 Fast & Easy®
0-7615-3395-8
U.S. $18.99 • Can. $28.95 • U.K. £13.99

Microsoft® Excel 2002 Fast & Easy®
0-7615-3398-2
U.S. $18.99 • Can. $28.95 • U.K. £13.99

Microsoft® FrontPage® 2002 Fast & Easy®
0-7615-3390-7
U.S. $18.99 • Can. $28.95 • U.K. £13.99

Microsoft® Office XP Fast & Easy®
0-7615-3388-5
U.S. $18.99 • Can. $28.95 • U.K. £13.99

Microsoft® Outlook 2002 Fast & Easy®
0-7615-3422-9
U.S. $18.99 • Can. $28.95 • U.K. £13.99

Microsoft® PowerPoint® 2002 Fast & Easy®
0-7615-3396-6
U.S. $18.99 • Can. $28.95 • U.K. £13.99

Microsoft® Word 2002 Fast & Easy®
0-7615-3393-1
U.S. $18.99 • Can. $28.95 • U.K. £13.99

PRIMA TECH
A Division of Prima Publishing
www.prima-tech.com

Call now to order
(800)632-8676 ext. 4444

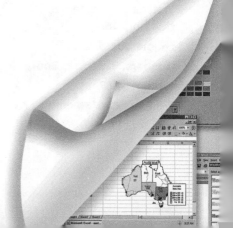

Prima Publishing and Fast & Easy are registered trademarks of Prima Communications, Inc.
All other product and company names are trademarks of their respective companies.